Copyright © 2023 by Frontline Church
All rights reserved.
First edition January 2023
Design by Jesse Owen, 10AM Design (*10am.org*)
ISBN 9798372052529
Published by Frontline Church
www.frontlinechurch.com

ACKNOWLEDGMENTS

We want to express our deep gratitude for the leadership of Frontline Church and the various contributions they have made throughout this process. This is an incredible team and we regularly thank the Lord for the opportunity to lock arms and multiply gospel communities that love God, love people, and push back darkness together.

Additionally, we want to thank The Village Church and the Austin Stone for providing resources from their Home Group Manual and Missional Community Leaders Field Guide, respectively. We are grateful for their partnership in the gospel.

FRONTLINE MISSION

*Multiplying gospel communities
that love God, love people,
and push back darkness*

INTRODUCTION

Frontline's Community Group Handbook is specifically designed to serve anyone involved in our community groups. This handbook aims to provide a clear vision for our groups, as well as answer common questions. Like any other handbook, it can't provide everything you'll need to know, but we hope it gives you a framework and a toolbox as you embark on the journey of life in community. In particular, this handbook is divided into three main sections:

COMMUNITY GROUPS

The first section of the handbook gives a general overview of community groups. It is specifically aimed at serving community group members who are wanting to learn more about why we have and how we do community groups. It provides a brief description of the goals and rhythms of community groups. If you or someone in your group is wanting to learn more about why we do what we do, this section would serve you best.

COMMUNITY GROUP LEADERSHIP

The second section of the handbook focuses on community group leadership. It is specifically aimed at serving existing community group leaders, or those who are considering community group leadership in the future. We provide a detailed description of what we expect of community group leaders, as well as practical outlines for apprenticeship and multiplication. We conclude by answering a few of the most commonly asked questions around leading a group.

DISCIPLESHIP GROUPS, FAMILY MEALS, MISSIONAL GATHERINGS

The final section of the handbook goes in-depth on each of our three rhythms of community groups. While anyone in a group would benefit from this section, it is designed to help community group leaders lead each of these rhythms. We cover why we do each of these, what they look like, and how to practically gather in these rhythms. Once again, we end each section by answering some of the most frequently asked questions around each rhythm.

Whether you are a group member, an apprentice, or a leader, our prayer is that this handbook will serve you well as you learn to love God, love people, and push back darkness in and through community.

COMMUNITY GROUPS

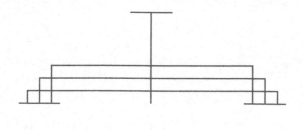

The biggest problem people have in searching for the perfect community is just that. You don't find community; you create it through love. Look how this transforms the way you enter a room full of strangers. Our instinctive thought is, "Who do I know? Who am I comfortable with?" There's nothing wrong with those questions, but the Jesus questions that create communities are, "Who can I love? Who is left out?" Here are two different formulas for community formation: 1) Search for community where I am loved [and] become disappointed with community, [or] 2) Show [God's] love [and] create community.

PAUL MILLER
A Loving Life

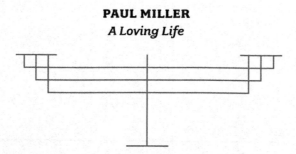

WHY COMMUNITY GROUPS?

In April of 1992, after years of withdrawing from society, Chris McCandless hitchhiked to Alaska and started down a snow-covered trail into the backcountry, carrying a bag of rice and a rifle, alone. After managing to survive on his own for more than 100 days, he died alone in an abandoned bus in the Alaskan wilderness. Whatever Chris McCandless was searching for on his own, he didn't think he'd find it in community.

Near his body, they found a copy of the Russian novel *Dr. Zhivago*. In it, he had highlighted a sentence and written a few words of his own in the margin. The sentence read: "And so it turned out that only a life similar to the life of those around us, merging with it without a ripple, is genuine life, and that an unshared happiness is not happiness." In the margin next to those words, McCandless had written in capital letters: HAPPINESS ONLY REAL WHEN SHARED.

WE WERE MADE FOR COMMUNITY

God designed us in such a way that happiness is only real when it's shared. We were made for community. Deep within us, there is a desire to belong to something bigger than ourselves. This desire is the driving motivation behind every club, team, social group, and even places we eat and buy groceries. But that desire is more than a mere social construct; it's in our very DNA.

The God who created us has eternally existed in community as Father, Son, and Holy Spirit. This Triune God created us in his image, with a longing for this kind of community and relationship. When sin entered the world, our relationship with God and each other was fractured. But since the beginning, God has been working to redeem and restore what was lost. And one day, people from every tribe, tongue, race, and nation will gather to worship and experience communion with God and each other

once again. With our future hope in view, followers of Jesus pursue community in the here and now.

If that's true, why do so many Christians still walk alone? Why is it so hard for us to move towards each other? Some of us are prone to believe the lie of self-reliance: *I don't need you*. Others of us are prone to believe the lie of worthlessness: *You don't need me*. These obstacles to community can at times seem insurmountable. Pride always draws us away from interdependence towards the illusion of self-reliance. If Pride could talk, it would probably say something like "I don't need you, I can do it myself."

As a result, we've become increasingly lonely, and it's even affecting us physically. Doctors are finding that loneliness causes "an insidious type of stress" that leads to chronic inflammation and an increased risk of heart disease, arthritis, and diabetes. Several large studies even claim that loneliness has the same effect on mortality as smoking fifteen cigarettes a day. But the good news is we don't have to walk alone.

WE ARE ONE BODY IN CHRIST

We can move towards each other, despite our pride, because we've been permanently joined together into one body by Jesus. We can move towards each other because we already belong.

> *For as in one body we have many members, and the members do not all have the same function, so we, though many, are one body in Christ, and individually members one of another. (Rom 12:4-5)*

We do not all have the same function, and we might not feel like we fit in. But in Christ, we do belong. Every Christian is not only unique, but uniquely needed. God has designed community in such a way that when we show up, we're all guaranteed to have something to offer! We are empowered by the Spirit of God to bless and serve others.

Having gifts that differ according to the grace given to us, let us use them: if prophecy, in proportion to our faith; if service, in our serving; the one who teaches, in his teaching; the one who exhorts, in his exhortation; the one who contributes, in generosity; the one who leads, with zeal; the one who does acts of mercy, with cheerfulness. (Rom 12:6-8)

God has designed his Body in such a way that when he acts to give us something we need, he tends to accomplish that primarily by giving it to others instead. When someone needs an encouraging word, God will spontaneously call it to someone else's mind and prompt them to share it. When someone is unable to discern the right choice, God will enable someone else to give them wise counsel. When someone is in danger of falling into sin, God will send others to ask good questions, listen, pray, and offer gentle correction. We all have something for our fellow Christians, and they need it.

LOVING GOD, LOVING PEOPLE, AND PUSHING BACK DARKNESS IN COMMUNITY

The Mission of Frontline Church is **multiplying gospel communities that love God, love people, and push back darkness**. One of the primary ways we do this is through community groups.

As we gather in community groups, we are invited to grow in our love for God. Our love for God is a response to his love for us. Through the gospel, we see the markers of God's overflowing love clearly displayed. God shows the depths of his love by sending Jesus to reconcile us back to him. Our love is always a response to his love. "In this is love, not that we have loved God but that he loved us and sent his Son to be the propitiation for our sins... We love because he first loved us" (1 Jn 4:10, 19).

As we gather in community groups, we are invited to grow in our love for each other. Just as Jesus loved and served us, we love and serve each other. John warns us against merely expressing our love "in word or talk but [not] in deed and in truth" (1 Jn 3:18). In community, we love one another by caring for one another. Our needs are uncovered and met as we walk together.

As we gather in community groups, we are invited to push back darkness around us. We gather, not just for ourselves, but for our communities. God has a mission to restore and redeem this world. And he sends us out to bring the light of the gospel to those in darkness and without hope. Our neighborhoods provide numerous opportunities to advance God's mission in our city.

OBSTACLES TO COMMUNITY

If we have tried community and come away disappointed, it may have been because too many of us were hiding in plain sight. If we've been disappointed, let's not lose heart and conclude that real Christian community is just a pipe dream. Open yourself up to being pleasantly surprised by the possibility of Christian community.

Other times we've tried community and come away disappointed because, in hindsight, we realized we were approaching it passively, like consumers. Paul Miller writes:

> *The biggest problem Christians have in searching for community is just that. You don't find community; you create it through love.*

As Tim Keller has pointed out, the single greatest factor that will determine your experience of Christian community is your experiential knowledge of God's love for you. If you find yourself having a hard time believing his love for you in a real and lasting way, there is an invitation for you to see Jesus in new and fresh ways. For our sake Jesus gave up his community. It's only because Jesus chose to be forsaken by his community that we can ever hope to have community with each other. In his pain, he hung alone, so that in our pain we might hang together. He willingly suffered alone in the dark in order to make sure that we can always walk together in the light of his love. *Happiness only real when shared.*

If you find yourself tempted to be cynical or dismissive about Christian community, think harder about the cross. We won't see the beauty of this community until we see the ugliness of that cross. Until we see what it cost to create this community, we will either treat it like it's so cheap it's not worth our time, or like it's so fragile it's only a matter of time before it betrays us. But in true Christian community, we have an opportunity to share the joy we find in Jesus.

WHAT ARE COMMUNITY GROUPS?

Local, diverse gospel communities that gather regularly for discipleship, care, and mission through discipleship groups, family meals, and missional gatherings

LOCAL

Community groups gather in homes around the city throughout the week. As we gather with other believers in our geographical area, we are able to make a deeper impact on the neighbors around us. We don't construct community groups on the basis of age, affinity, or interest. Instead, our community groups are geographical, comprised of people who live in a similar region and context. In his earthly life, Jesus emphasized the importance of offering presence to those around us. In the same way, our community groups are rooted in a local community, seeking to love and serve our real-life neighbors.

DIVERSE

Ideally, community groups contain people from all different backgrounds, ethnicities, and stages of life. They are intergenerational and diverse. Community groups are not merely a Sunday school class, a social action club, or a support group. We don't gather in community because of shared hobbies or interests. Rather, as we gather together with people who are different from us, we are able to see things we've never seen before. In the Church, Jesus has sought to reconcile people who were divided by all kinds of barriers, whether political, racial, or socioeconomic. Our community groups welcome people from all walks of life to experience the transforming power of the gospel.

GOSPEL COMMUNITIES

Community groups, along with our five congregations, our one church, and our church plants, are all "gospel communities." Gospel communities are distinct from other kinds of groups in that they are committed to the gospel and to one another. Gospel communities are together:

- *Because of Jesus*—gathering because of our hope in Jesus rather than hobbies, stage of life, or culture
- *With Jesus*—being empowered for ministry and mission by the Holy Spirit
- *Under Jesus*—following him in what he has spoken to us through the Scriptures
- *For Jesus*—passionately seeking the good of our city and longing for more people to meet Jesus

Ultimately, Jesus is the one who unites us and gives us meaning as a group.

THAT GATHER REGULARLY

A community group is more than a weekly meeting. Instead, in a healthy community group, people increasingly live their lives together in order to increasingly pursue Jesus together. In so doing, they resemble the kind of community we see in Acts 2.

And they devoted themselves to the apostles' teaching and to the fellowship, to the breaking of bread and the prayers. And awe came upon every soul, and many wonders and signs were being done through the apostles. And all who believed were together and had all things in common. And they were selling their possessions and belongings and distributing the proceeds to all, as any had need. And day by day, attending the temple together and breaking bread in their homes, they received their food with glad and generous hearts, praising God and having favor with all the people. And the Lord added to their number day by day those who were being saved. (Acts 2:42-47)

THE GOALS OF COMMUNITY GROUPS

At Frontline, our community groups love God, love people, and push back darkness through discipleship, care, and mission.

DISCIPLESHIP

Discipleship is the process where, by the power of the Spirit, we are being made more like Jesus in every area of our life. When we follow Jesus, we are called into a life of discipleship. Through the gospel, we continually work to know and follow Jesus, as the Spirit works powerfully in us (Phil 1:6; 2:13). The more we look to Jesus, the more we'll look like Jesus. The good news of Jesus is both a message we proclaim and a power at work in us.

As we follow Jesus together, we are called to disciple one another (Eph 4:11-16). We are continually in need of grace. We point one another to the good news of Jesus—that while we are more sinful than we dared feared, we are more loved than we dared hope. We encourage one another to put away sin and to run after Jesus. Discipleship happens in everyday life, as we live in community and on mission together. We get to know one another, our struggles and victories, our fears and hopes. Community groups help us disciple one another.

CARE

Care is the practice of loving one another. Jesus calls his followers to love others in the same way he loved us. We care for one another holistically, whether physically, spiritually, emotionally, or relationally. We care for one another as we help our friends and neighbors, deliver meals to new mothers, and pray for one another. We care by being relationally thoughtful and honoring others above ourselves. We care by offering our time and presence to those who are grieving. Sometimes, caring for others calls us to speak truth in love, to rebuke, to point people away from their sin to Jesus. Where we see the needy, the sick, the hurting, or the struggling, we seek to love them as Jesus loved us.

Care can rarely be accomplished by a single individual. The responsibility of care doesn't need to fall on one person or leader. Rather, we need a community of people who know us and love us to effectively care for us. When we experience seasons of care, we can most often have our needs met within the context of community. Community groups help us care for one another.

MISSION

Mission is our calling as a community—to know God and to make him known. Every follower of Jesus is called to be a missionary, to bring the good news of Jesus into the places they live, work, play, and study. God has placed us in our families, our jobs, and our neighborhoods to be the salty brightness of the transforming work of Jesus. When we were in darkness and without hope, Jesus came for us and laid down his life to rescue us. And so wherever we now find ourselves, we seek to bring the peace, presence, and life of Jesus to all creation. We feed the hungry and care for the sick. We know and meet the needs of our neighbors. We share the good news of Jesus with those who do not know him. People are not projects. As we share the gospel and live on mission, we truly care for people, learn their stories, and meet them with the same love that was shown to us.

We carry out our mission best in community. When we engage the mission of Jesus together, our resources multiply, and our effectiveness increases. We are better able to intercede, engage, and invite. As we live in frequent proximity with each other and our neighbors, we display the love of Jesus to a watching world. As community groups all over our city engage their neighbors with the good news of Jesus, we will reach people we never could through a Sunday gathering. Mission in community has the power to transform our city for the sake of the gospel. This will require every member to commit to live a missionary life on the six days between Sundays. Community groups help us live on mission together.

THE RHYTHMS OF COMMUNITY GROUPS

Frontline community groups have varied rhythms to match the rhythms of everyday life. Some settings naturally require a greater level of vulnerability and openness than others. For instance, a person may not be comfortable stepping into the intimacy of someone's living room, but they may be open to going to a neutral place where they meet new people who happen to be Christians. On the other hand, if a person's only experience of the church is in neutral places, they may never be confronted with the depth and messiness of Christian community. To that end, Frontline community groups gather in three regular rhythms— discipleship groups, family meals, and missional gatherings. Each rhythm has its own function and goal. Our hope is that through these three rhythms, we would see people come to know and trust Jesus in a deeper way.

DISCIPLESHIP GROUPS

> *Gender-specific groups of three or four who gather regularly to know and encourage one another in their walk with Jesus*

If community doesn't draw us deeper into discipleship, it will become just another way to hide in plain sight. A discipleship group is ideally formed from within a community group, though there are some exceptions to this. As we grow in trust and safety with one another, we will more effectively be able to disciple one another.

In a healthy, gospel-centered discipleship group, we remind each other that while we are more sinful than we dared feared, we are more loved than we dared hope. Together, we confess our sins, we point each other to Jesus, and we encourage each other to live in line with the gospel.

When a discipleship group gathers together, it typically includes four movements that help a group become more balanced, biblical, and fruitful.

1. Scripture. Briefly check in on your engagement with Scripture since your last gathering. What's one bit of Scripture you are applying to one bit of your life? One bit of Scripture can lead you to adore God, see and hate your sin, or ask for grace. To apply one bit of Scripture to one bit of your life requires at least meditation, if not memorization. If multiple of you are repeatedly showing up not having read your Bibles, make a shift in your discipleship group. Instead of continuing to answer the Scripture question in the negative, take 20 minutes at the beginning of your gathering to read Scripture together over the next several weeks. You can use the alternate Discipleship Group Guide, which outlines how to have a discipleship group in this way. You can find this guide in the "Discipleship Groups" section of this handbook or online at *frontlinechurch.com/discipleship.*

2. Sharing. Briefly check in personally. How is God changing you for the good (sanctification)? What are you facing that's hard (suffering)? What sin or temptation do you need to confess (sin)? Ed Welch notes that when someone confesses sin, we shouldn't simply commiserate. Instead, we should aim for the heart, work to develop a plan, and recognize the messy nature of growth and change. We should feel concerned if we can't identify our own temptations, and blessed if we can. For all of us, our goal should be to bring our sins out into the open and grow in saying "no" to sinful desires (Titus 2:11-12).

3. Spread of the Gospel. Remind the group of the names of your "three," and briefly check-in. How is it going pursuing and praying for them? Your goal should be to prayerfully name three people who don't follow Jesus within your sphere of influence. You will then commit to pray for and engage them in intentional gospel relationships. These people could be your children, family, friends, co-workers, neighbors, or others. Whom would you most love to see become a disciple of Jesus? Who is your heart best shaped to reach for Jesus? Naming and praying for your "three" every time you gather will guard your group against spiritual navel-gazing and self-obsession.

4. *Spirit-Filled Prayer.* After someone has shared, respond with Spirit-filled prayer. Possible signs we are inviting the Spirit into our prayers: (1) when our prayers comfortably move in and out of silence, (2) when we find ourselves praying more than once, and (3) when we pray Scripture, thoughts, pictures, and even gut impressions, spontaneously brought to mind by God. We should always filter these impressions through Scripture, as well as weigh and test them in wise community (1 Thess 5:21; 1 Cor 14:29).

For a more detailed look at discipleship groups, as well as answers to common questions, see the section entitled "Discipleship Groups" later in this handbook.

FAMILY MEALS

Casual gatherings around a common table for the sake of community and gospel hospitality

Real-life conversations happen in real-life situations. Some of the best conversations happen around the dinner table or while we're washing the dishes. For our family meals, we set aside an entire evening to prepare, eat, and clean up a meal together. As we linger over the meal, we listen, talk, and pray. Slowly, over time, we can become friends, and—on a deeper level—family. As we eat a meal together, we have the opportunity to experience true community. Participating in a meal together is a symbol of our fellowship and relationship with one another. If we are willing, we can learn one another's stories, vocations, and passions. Quite simply, we become a spiritual family as we practice the "one anothers" of Scripture.

At Frontline, our community groups typically meet for family meal twice a month, on the first and third week of the month. This gathering centers around the meal—preparing, eating, and cleaning up together as a community. A family meal will look different from one community group to the next. We may spend the evening praying for one

another. Sometimes, we may talk about what Jesus is teaching us or what we learned from the most recent sermon. And other times, we may just spend time getting to know one another better. However it looks, we pursue the same purpose: to live out our identity as a spiritual family.

At a family meal, we can invite friends, family, co-workers, and non-believers to meet our group and experience God's grace in a less intimidating setting. In pursuit of the Great Commission, we need other avenues for inviting people to experience Christian community besides simply inviting them to a Sunday worship gathering. While some people might be hesitant to set foot inside a church building, they are more likely to show up at a family meal and experience the love of Jesus. Mission is best carried out in the context of community.

For a more detailed look at family meals, as well as answers to common questions, see the section entitled "Family Meals" later in this handbook.

MISSIONAL GATHERINGS

Gathering intentionally for the sake of people far from God to proclaim the gospel and demonstrate the kingdom

In addition to our own growth and development, community groups exist so that others might come to know and follow Jesus. Missional gatherings help us push back darkness through both gospel proclamation and kingdom demonstration. Missional gatherings give us the opportunity to build relationships with those who don't follow Jesus and tell them about the one who has rescued us. They also give us the opportunity to care for the spiritual and physical needs of those in darkness around us. We gather missionally in three primary ways.

First, we gather missionally to host. We gather with the expressed intention of showing gospel hospitality to those outside of Christian community. Hospitality builds trust and encourages conversations to go deeper. Acquaintances might even become friends. Hosting could be as simple as throwing a block party or engaging some cultural event, such as Halloween or the Super Bowl. Or it could look like inviting one of your neighbors to your next family meal. Whatever it looks like, we hope that through hosting, our presence would begin to be felt in our neighborhood.

Second, we gather missionally to help. We prioritize serving with our city partners, which are organizations thoughtfully chosen by each congregation on the basis of their impact. As we serve the poor, marginalized, and needy in our communities, we build relationships with our community. Since many non-Christians also have a desire to do good for their city, we can invite them to serve alongside us as a means of strengthening our friendship. There are needs all around us, even right next door. As we thoughtfully engage where we live, we will notice people and places where we can bring the light of Jesus to the world. We provide Push Back Darkness Grants to our community groups to empower them to meet specific needs in their own community.

Finally, we gather missionally to hang out. We gather regularly with those who don't follow Jesus in natural, neutral places outside of the church and our homes. This helps us form new friendships and introduce people to Christian community, while we gather with people where they already are. This could be at a coffee shop, a park, a concert, or some other event. It could be centered around a hobby or another recreational activity. Regardless, the point is to look for less-intimidating places where we can build relationships with non-Christians. We should invite our unbelieving friends, family, and neighbors to gather with us as we have fun together and get to know one another. The hope is that through these missional gatherings, natural conversations will come up about Jesus and the hope we have in him.

For a more detailed look at missional gatherings, as well as answers to common questions, see the section entitled "Missional Gatherings" later in this handbook.

SCHEDULING RHYTHMS

Regular Community Group Rhythms. In order to engage all three rhythms of community groups, we do different things on different weeks. An ideal community group schedule might look like this:

- Week 1 - Family meal
- Week 2 - Discipleship groups
- Week 3 - Family meal
- Week 4 - Discipleship groups
- Week 5 - Group-wide missional gathering (typically four times per year)

Planning Missional Gatherings. Ideally, missional gatherings spontaneously happen on a smaller scale, with a few people in the group engaging their neighbors and friends. But occasionally, we should plan for a missional gathering that includes most of the group.

Avoid carrying the weight of missional planning alone. Ask someone in your group to regularly look ahead in the calendar. Consider what upcoming dates might create a missional opportunity. Keep an eye on moments like New Year's Eve, Super Bowl Sunday, Easter, Fourth of July, Halloween, Thanksgiving, Christmas, or any other cultural event that is important to the people around you. Make a plan for how your community group will engage these occasions, including potential missional gatherings you may schedule.

As a rule—for large-scale missional gatherings—planning ahead produces a better response than last-minute appeals. Group members are often more willing to say "yes" and show up than leaders might think. The earlier and more often leaders communicate both the vision and the plan, the better response they will typically get from their group members.

Summer and Winter Break. Community groups typically take two breaks each year in July and December, which are natural moments for people to scatter on vacation or holiday. Leaders should use this time to recuperate and regain vision for the next semester. During these breaks, community group members will often still spend relaxed time together, but the leaders are released from the responsibility of organizing and leading those gatherings. The summer and winter breaks are an ideal time for community groups to multiply.

COMMUNITY GROUP STRUCTURE

HUBS

> *Two to four community groups connected geographically for more efficient mission, more effective pastoral care, and more exact equipping*

Our community groups are organized into "hubs." Each hub is overseen by hub leaders who cast vision, coach, and provide pastoral care for both the hub's group leaders and group members. As a hub, community groups collaborate together to engage a specific area of their city. Occasionally, a hub will gather for training or deeper community.

LEADERSHIP TEAM

Healthy community groups require healthy structures of support. At Frontline Church, our leadership structure for community groups looks like this:

Community Director. Each congregation has a community director that is responsible for the direction and health of community groups at their congregation. They oversee, coach, and develop the hub leaders in their congregation.

Hub Leader. Hub leaders are responsible for the direction and health of their hub. They oversee, coach, and develop the community group leaders within their hub. Each hub has a male and female hub leader, and may have other leaders as a part of the hub leadership team.

Community Group Leader. A community group leader is responsible for the direction and health of their community group. They oversee, coach, and develop the apprentices within their group. For more on what a community group leader does and how to become a community group leader, see the "What Is a Community Group Leader?" section in this handbook.

Apprentice. Apprentices are potential community group leaders. Whether formally or informally, they are being equipped to lead as they are gradually given responsibility within the group. An apprentice helps shoulder the load alongside of, and under, the direction of their leaders. For more on what apprenticeship looks like, see the "Apprenticeship" section in this handbook.

COMMUNITY GROUP LEADERSHIP

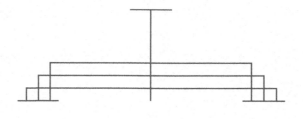

Among the followers of Jesus... leadership is not a synonym for lordship. Our calling is to be servants not bosses, slaves not masters. True, a certain authority attaches to all leaders, and leadership would be impossible without it... Yet the emphasis of Jesus was not on the authority of a ruler-leader but on the humility of a servant-leader. The authority by which the Christian leader leads is not power but love, not force but example, not coercion but reasoned persuasion. Leaders have power, but power is safe only in the hands of those who humble themselves to serve.

JOHN STOTT
Issues Facing Christians Today

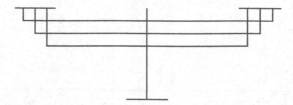

WHAT IS A COMMUNITY GROUP LEADER?

Community group leaders serve a vital role in our church. A community group leader is responsible for the direction and health of their community group. They oversee, coach, and develop the apprentices within their group. For this reason, there are certain requirements for community group leaders.

REQUIREMENTS FOR A COMMUNITY GROUP LEADER

The following requirements must be met for someone to be considered for community group leadership:

- *A believing and baptized Christian*
- *A covenant member in good standing with the church*
- *Completion of the launch process found at* frontlinechurch.com/launch

COMMUNITY GROUP LEADER JOB DESCRIPTION

Does the thought of leading a community group make you nervous? You're not alone. Like most people, you might be carrying a confusing and contradictory tangle of ideas about leadership that swirl in the culture at large. You might think to yourself: "I'm not a leader—leaders should be charismatic and outgoing, and always know what to do. On top of all that, to lead in the church you need to be armed with ready-made answers to every conceivable biblical question."

Or, like many others, you might be carrying bad memories of previous leadership experiences. You might think to yourself: "My experience of leadership has always been lonely and exhausting, but I keep getting sucked back in because nobody else will step up."

If you can relate to any of that, good news! Our community group leaders don't have all the answers either. They are not afraid to say, "I don't know, but I'll get back to you," because they know their pastors and hub leaders will help them find the answers they need. Our community group leaders have wildly diverse personality types and talents, and they have been relieved to discover they don't have to lead alone.

Community group leadership is both easier and harder than you might think. Easier because at Frontline character and commitment always trump charisma and copious knowledge. Harder because refusing to lead alone, asking for help, saying "I don't know," listening more than talking, and patiently walking alongside others are not behaviors any of us have seen modeled enough. Our community group leaders are normal people, just like you, who quietly and patiently walk alongside, listen to, pray for, and follow up with others—and they do all of those things for people *with* people, as a team.

If you are willing, set aside your preconceptions, assumptions, and fears about leadership for a moment, and see if the following five commitments don't stir something in your heart. Here is the real "job description" of a Frontline community group leader:

- *A commitment to co-labor*
- *A commitment to communicate*
- *A commitment to pursue*
- *A commitment to mature*
- *A commitment to champion*

1. A COMMITMENT TO CO-LABOR

Most people assume community group leadership is inherently lonely, but lonely community group leadership is not sustainable leadership. Scripture describes being saved out of the world as simultaneously being saved into a family. All of us have been given spiritual gifts to build each other up, but none of us have been given all the gifts. Because Jesus has designed the Church to function interdependently, we are committed to team ministry at Frontline. When leaders feel weary, overwhelmed, and lonely, they tend to think "It'll be easier if I just do it myself."

Counter-intuitively, a large part of leadership is learning to ask for help, give up control, and share the load. We might go faster alone, but we'll go farther together. Team ministry moves far slower, but it's far more sustainable.

Ask for help. Identify others' gifting and energy in the areas of planning, hosting, communication, and facilitation. Invite them in. Give up control in order to gain help. Don't get discouraged when their help doesn't meet your standards the first time around. Gently and calmly give them direct and immediate feedback, and watch them grow in using their gifts to support you and bless the group.

Healthy community group leaders aren't Lone Rangers who do everything themselves. Instead, they constantly think and preach "team," and work alongside others to help their group grow in maturity. Rather than taking on every role within their group, they delegate tasks and call others to relate to the group like owners, not renters. They also welcome and seek out coaching, advice, and soul care from their hub leaders.

A commitment to co-labor might look like...

- making a list of everything that's needed for your group to be healthy and run smoothly, and asking yourself who might be good at stewarding each of those tasks (creating and communicating the group calendar, planning the family meals, hosting, facilitating a d-group, planning and coordinating a missional gathering, setting up a meal calendar for a new mom, leading a service project for an elderly group member, etc.).

- prayerfully reading through the "Apprenticeship" section of this handbook in order to strengthen your ability to identify, equip, and launch others.

- identifying and recruiting another person or couple to apprentice.

2. A COMMITMENT TO COMMUNICATE

Communication is a key part of co-laboring. Lone Ranger leaders don't tend to be great communicators. Your group members will feel cared for and led well whenever you proactively develop and communicate the plan for the upcoming schedule. Share the load of planning and communication to ensure it happens consistently. Just because you are responsible to make sure everything gets done doesn't mean you should do everything.

Communication isn't just for logistics—it's also for relationship. One of the biggest keys to success as a community group leader is working to slowly build trust over time with your hub leader. As you get more comfortable with them, you can let them know more and more about what you're thinking and feeling. In turn they can encourage you and pray for you in increasingly thoughtful ways. Can you name what you are afraid of? What you are avoiding? Share with your hub leader—it will lighten you. "We name things to tame things."

A commitment to communicate might look like...

- sitting down with your fellow leaders and apprentices to map out dates, times, and locations for family meals and discipleship groups for the next 60 to 90 days. Once you're done, have someone who's handy with that kind of thing lay it all out in a clean and clear format and send it out to the group.

- recruiting someone to send out week-of and day-of reminders to the group before each gathering, as well as choose the themes, and coordinate the preparation, for all family meals.

- recruiting someone to collect everyone's contact information (phone numbers, addresses, birthdays, names of children, etc.), and then distribute all the information to the group. They can also set up a group text or email thread, as well as take the initiative to regularly update the group's communication channels whenever new members join the group. Ask them to alert you whenever a group member's birthday is approaching, as well as help facilitate a way to recognize and celebrate that person.

3. A COMMITMENT TO PURSUE

Community group leaders are not called to merely set out chips and salsa and keep the conversation going. Community group leaders are called to walk alongside other people as spiritual friends and fellow travelers, in order to get to know them well enough to pray for them. Indeed, all forms of "pursuit" are simply variations on the theme of knowing people well enough to pray for them.

Only God is all-knowing, all-powerful, and everywhere-at-once. You won't be able to answer all their questions, fix all their problems, or be there for them all the time. But you can always listen, encourage, and pray. You can always ask thoughtful questions. You can always notice when they're absent, and let them know they were missed. You can always follow up after a meaningful conversation, ask how they're doing, and let them know they've been on your mind. In fact, the majority of your ministry as a community group leader will involve offering your peaceful, prayerful presence, and then following up.

A commitment to pursue might look like...

- taking a few moments after a meaningful conversation to stop and write down significant details before you forget them (names of family members, significant life events, etc.). The notes section of their contact card in your phone is a great spot that can be easily pulled up or added to.

- setting a reminder in your calendar to pray for someone before a big event in their life, as well as calling them afterwards to hear how it went. Or setting a reminder for yourself to call and pray for someone when you know they'll be on a business trip and struggling with loneliness or temptation.

- casting vision for how every member can take personal initiative to move towards others, and check-in, listen, pray, and otherwise be human with each other during unstructured time

together. This is particularly applicable to the family meal.

- asking an appropriate, trusted person in your group to check in on someone who's been absent or has a need.

4. A COMMITMENT TO MATURE

We don't necessarily invite people to consider community group leadership because they're brimming with leadership confidence. We invite them because they're brimming with character, and seem to possess a sense of calling to this unique ministry—the kind of calling that will keep them from bailing out the minute it gets hard. Competence can be coached on the job, but character and calling are prerequisites. That's the paradox of leadership—sometimes the people who feel the least qualified are the most qualified! Pride might keep someone from growing as a leader, but fear could keep them from ever becoming one in the first place—especially if they wrongly assume they have to be a Bible expert, trauma specialist, public speaker, or visionary thought leader (whatever that is).

Again, character is a prerequisite for community group leadership, and perhaps the most unmistakable mark of character is humility—the kind of realistic view of ourselves that makes us teachable, receptive, and willing to grow.

Spiritual maturity is not a destination at which any of us have arrived, but a direction in which we're all headed. One sign that we are growing in maturity is if we can name—with help from our friends—at least one place where we sense an invitation from Jesus to grow and change.

- Jonathan is more likely to: hide his flaws, avoid challenges, and view feedback as a personal attack.

- Kristen is more likely to: believe mistakes are part of learning, embrace challenges, and welcome feedback.

Would those closest to you say you're more like Jonathan or Kristen?

Community group leadership requires patience with yourself and patience with your group. You can expect to make mistakes. What matters most is how you respond. Don't beat yourself up over every little mistake. Rather, as you fix your eyes on Jesus, you will stop thinking less of yourself, and start to think of yourself less. God will faithfully lead you into radical "extrospection," where you navel-gaze less, and move towards others more. Paul describes this progression as "love that issues from a pure heart and a good conscience and a sincere faith" (1 Tim 1:5).

This kind of humble receptivity is enabled and sustained only by genuine spiritual vitality—including regular rhythms of communing with God through Scripture and prayer. If that doesn't feel true of your present reality, begin cultivating new habits that will sustain you on the journey. For help with engaging Scripture, see additional resources in our Leadership Library (*frontlinechurch.com/library*).

At Frontline, every ministry role invests in your development as a follower of Jesus before it's ever about what you can do for that ministry. We are committed to using ministry to build up people, rather than using people to build up ministry.

A commitment to mature might look like...

- fighting to regularly find your joy and comfort in the Lord—through Scripture, prayer, and fresh in-fillings of the Spirit.

- taking the initiative to ask for help on the front end, and feedback on the back end, instead of avoiding it, or merely bracing for it.

- learning to tell yourself a different story when you make mistakes, by actively naming how each mistake has created an opportunity for you to strengthen a weakness, deepen your character, or learn a new skill.

5. A COMMITMENT TO CHAMPION

Every local church has its own way of doing things—the ministry practices by which they seek to live out the mission God has given them. And every church must agree on a particular kind of discipleship strategy, so they can all head in the same direction with one heart and mind. At Frontline, community groups play an essential role in how we do ministry. We've chosen to gather our community groups in

three different rhythms: discipleship groups, family meals, and missional gatherings. These three rhythms are not sacred or inherently superior to any other model. Other churches may do things differently with great success. But we believe these rhythms are the best way for us to love God, love people, and push back darkness in this time and place.

Community group leaders must be willing to champion these rhythms and how we seek to walk them out. They cannot half-heartedly run these plays, or pull their group in a different direction from the rest of our church. Leaders who spend more energy complaining about the model than capitalizing on its strengths will miss out on countless opportunities to disciple their people. If all our groups are on the same page, rowing in the same direction, and working from the same plan, our people will generally experience growth and health, despite the inherent imperfection of any and every ministry strategy. Leaders need to believe in our model, cast vision for why it matters, and call their people to commit to living it out with them.

A commitment to champion might look like...

- carefully reading through the section of this handbook entitled "The Rhythms of Community Groups" in order to gain a better understanding of both the "why" and "what" of each rhythm.

- identifying and naming any internal resistance towards, or confusion about, any of the three rhythms you might feel—and then giving your community director the opportunity to speak with you in person about your resistance or confusion.

- being well-versed in not just the limitations and imperfections of our model, but also its benefits, advantages, and unique opportunities.

HOW DO I BECOME A COMMUNITY GROUP LEADER?

New community group leaders are identified and equipped by existing group leaders and hub leaders, particularly through our apprenticeship process. If you have a desire to lead a group and haven't been approached yet, reach out to your group leader about becoming an apprentice.

When hub leaders and group leaders decide an apprentice is ready to be assessed and launched, they will invite that apprentice to walk through the following six steps (also found at *frontlinechurch. com/launch*).

1. *Watch the community group leader training videos.* You can find these videos online at *frontlinechurch.com/launch*. These videos will lay the groundwork for your time as a community group leader.

2. *Complete the Gospel Self-Assessment*. You can find this online assessment at *frontlinechurch. com/launch*. If you already filled out the Gospel Self-Assessment as part of your apprenticeship process, you do not need to fill it out again.

3. *Meet with your community director and hub leaders for an assessment.* Once you've submitted the Gospel Self-Assessment, your community director will reach out to set up this meeting. Afterwards, if your leaders feel you are ready to step into this role, you will be provided with next steps.

4. *Complete MinistrySafe's Sexual Abuse Awareness Training.* Before becoming a community group leader, every candidate must be in compliance with Frontline's MinistrySafe Sexual Abuse Awareness Training policy. Your community director will let you know how to proceed.

5. *Get commissioned on a Sunday.* This is an opportunity for the church to pray over you as your community group prepares to launch, but it's also a chance for you to do some free advertising! Formally request to be commissioned, and make sure all the details for your new group are locked in (e.g., launch date, time, place, etc.) by filling out the Launch Checklist, which can be found at *frontlinechurch.com/launch*.

6. *Gather your group and go through Basic Training.* As you step into leadership, your group will be equipped with Frontline's Basic Training curriculum.

APPRENTICESHIP

The term "apprenticeship" refers to a method of training where a skilled worker passes on the practical knowledge they have acquired over the years. The apprentice receives one-on-one training, hands-on practice, and an opportunity to see the skills needed to succeed. The benefit of this method is that it allows our learning to move out of theory and into reality. It is one thing to read a textbook about a medical procedure; it is another thing entirely to perform that procedure under the watchful eye of a knowledgeable and caring mentor, with an opportunity to ask questions and receive feedback.

In our community groups, we take an apprenticeship approach to leadership development. This means we don't just train new community group leaders in a classroom or on a screen. Rather, we ask each of our group leaders to take on an apprentice, in order to relationally pass on the knowledge they have acquired in their experience as a leader. In doing so, apprenticeship moves leadership out of theory and into reality. It is a form of development with dirt under its fingernails.

In addition, apprenticeship allows us to not solely focus on techniques, but to aim for mature followers of Jesus marked by wisdom. Our hope is that, through apprenticeship, a person would grow as a disciple and deepen their understanding of how God can use them in the lives of others. The primary goal of apprenticeship is not to increase our number of community groups. The primary goal is "that we may present everyone mature in Christ" (Col 1:28).

WHAT IS AN APPRENTICE?

Apprentices are potential community group leaders. Whether formally or informally, they are being equipped to lead and gradually given responsibility within the group. An apprentice helps shoulder the load alongside of and under the direction of their leaders. Depending on their skill and experience, apprentices are the most likely people to lead a multiplication out of their group. Every community group should have an apprentice as soon as possible. Not every apprentice will become a group leader. But the hope is that every apprentice would deepen their joy in Jesus as they serve and learn alongside their leaders.

HOW DO I LEAD AN APPRENTICE?

As a community group leader, one of your major responsibilities is to identify, equip, and launch leaders. Therefore, we ask that every leader commit to recruit one or two apprentices. You are encouraged to do this from the start of your group, preferably within the first 90 days. This process requires us to be intentional—prayerfully asking God to raise up new leaders, and diligently working towards their development. Consider the following as a guide:

1. Identifying an Apprentice

Over the last several weeks, you've begun to notice leadership potential in John and Cindy. Every time someone new visits the group, they have been hospitable and made the person feel welcome. They also have been quick to pray for others when someone shares a need with the group. You're not quite sure they would make good community group leaders, or even if they would want to. But when you think of who you would trust to lead a group, they are the first ones that come to mind.

While there's no absolute formula for identifying an apprentice, there are several qualities to look for.

- Who is consistently present?
- Who engages discussion (not dominating the conversation, but contributing meaningfully)?
- Who helps meet the needs of the group?

- Who is especially hospitable?
- Who has expressed a willingness to step into leadership?

Someone does not have to check all the boxes above before we start the apprenticeship conversation with them. Still, markers like these can help alert us to potential apprentices. Make sure you don't simply look for someone like you. The body of Christ is immensely diverse, and so are those whom he has called as leaders. Be open to consider people who are very different from you.

If you are struggling to identify a possible apprentice in your group, that's okay. It can be difficult to recognize leadership potential in others. Ask your hub leader for input. They may have a different perspective on the members of your group as they have visited your group and gotten to know the members better. But more importantly, pray regularly for God to raise up leaders and give you discernment (Matt 9:27-28).

2. Inviting an Apprentice

"Greg, I really appreciate how you contribute to our community group, especially by driving us to be better about engaging our neighborhood. I think there could be some real leadership gifts in your life. Would you consider stepping into some more responsibility in our community group? In particular, I'd love it if you planned our next missional gathering and helped us serve and engage our neighbors."

Apprenticeship typically begins informally, asking an individual to begin taking on some leadership responsibilities in the group. You could begin by letting a person know that you have observed certain leadership qualities in them and invite them to begin taking on some responsibilities for the group. This could look like coordinating events, scheduling meals, sending group communication, leading a discussion, or attending a training. This allows an individual to get a feel for leadership, find their gifting, and clarify their calling. This unofficial stage creates less stress than formally naming someone an "apprentice" and also gives the leader a chance to evaluate and equip without pressure.

In time, some will begin to show themselves as candidates for more formal apprenticeship. At this point, the community group leader should ask the person to become an apprentice in hopes to train them to lead a community group one day. Some people may sense a call to leadership, but never step into it if you don't invite them in. Having spent time informally with them, they should be more confident to take on greater responsibility. At this point, there are a few things to invite them to do:

- Read a copy of this Community Group Handbook. Ask them to read a section at a time and discuss with you.
- Fill out the Gospel Self-Assessment and Reality Check Self-Assessment. They can find these online at *frontlinechurch.com/library*. As they complete each assessment, they can forward you their results and schedule a time to process in person.
- Begin attending your Hub Leadership Gatherings. These are regular meetings with your hub leaders and the other community group leaders in your hub for training and connection. These gatherings will help shape the apprentice's understanding of gospel community and Frontline culture.

If your invitation is met with hesitation or "no," don't panic. Ask follow-up questions with a posture of calm curiosity. As you process with them, you may realize there is a misunderstanding of what apprenticeship entails, or some previous experience in Christian community that is haunting them. Be patient and give them time to think and pray about your conversation. In other instances, there may be legitimate reasons they shouldn't step into apprenticeship at this time. Either way, if they are persistent, respect their "no." You can still assign small, informal responsibilities to them, as they are willing.

3. Equipping an Apprentice

Karen is showing a lot of progress as you talk about community group leadership. But she lacks confidence in her ability to lead a group discussion. You ask Karen to lead the next women's discipleship group while you participate. You give her the Discipleship Group Guide and tell her what you have learned as you've led that time. You remind her that you'll have her back if something unexpected comes up during the group, but that you would like her to take the lead. You meet up the following week to give feedback and encouragement.

If someone has accepted our invitation into apprenticeship, we have a responsibility to prayerfully help them identify a few places Jesus might be inviting them to grow. We need to thoughtfully build out a plan to help develop them as a leader and follower of Jesus. If we neglect that responsibility, we may end up inadvertently using them to build up ministry instead of using ministry to build them up. We should be looking for areas that need attention in our apprentice's life and leadership, whether theological, philosophical, or practical.

In particular, you should guide them through our Apprenticeship Training Plan (*frontlinechurch. com/apprenticeship*). The Apprenticeship Training Plan is a tool to help you equip your apprentice in the five commitments of community group leadership. As they complete each step, ask them to initiate a conversation with you to discuss what they are learning, as well as forwarding any online assessments they fill out. Be sure that you are listening intently during these conversations and making note of specific areas your apprentice needs to grow. Review these prior to each subsequent meeting. This is a great opportunity to give them additional resources for development, some of which can be found in our Leadership Library (*frontlinechurch.com/library*). Ask your hub leader for any book, sermon, or article recommendations that fall outside the scope of the Leadership Library.

In addition, you should provide them with more responsibility in the leadership of the community group, while providing encouragement and feedback. We don't want to give someone more than they can handle, but we do want to provide them with opportunities to stretch themselves. We want to give them a safe place to try things out, grow, and maybe even fail. Areas where we might delegate responsibility include:

- Facilitating discussion during a discipleship group or family meal
- Praying for a hurting person in their discipleship group
- Coordinating the meal calendar for family meal

- Praying for the group before you eat at family meal
- Planning and leading a missional gathering
- Handling the weekly communication with the rest of the group
- Setting up a Meal Train for someone in need of care
- Meeting up with a member of the community group to check in on them

It is important in each of these areas to give feedback to the apprentice, sharing the things you have learned from experience as you have led the group.

4. Assessing an Apprentice

Michael and Janet have been serving as apprentices for the last seven months. They have been working through the Apprenticeship Training Plan and occasionally leading various aspects of the community group, such as leading discussion and handling communication. In consultation with your hub leader, you feel like it is time for your group to multiply and for Michael and Janet to become community group leaders. "Michael and Janet, I think it's time for you to start praying about leading a group that multiplies out of our existing group. I'd like to sit down with you and process calling, further growth, and next steps."

As you invest in your apprentice, it is important to regularly assess when your apprentice is ready to step into leading their own community group. Part of this assessment will include evaluating your group's readiness to multiply. You can find more information on multiplication and how to lead your group through it in the section entitled "Multiplication" in this handbook. Your hub leader will help you assess when the time is right for multiplication, taking into account a number of factors include the readiness of your apprentices. But in general, your apprentice may be ready to move towards community group leadership if they have done the following:

- Accepted your invitation to formal apprenticeship
- Aspired to group leadership
- Worked through any growth areas in the Apprenticeship Training Plan

- Gotten experience in leading aspects of your community group
- Regularly met with you for coaching and ongoing development

When you and your hub leader feel it is time to move forward, invite your apprentice to begin the launch process (*frontlinechurch.com/launch*). This process will still give time for you, your hub leader, and your apprentice to address areas of growth and cast a vision for multiplication to your group. You can find more information on this process under the section entitled "How Do I Become a Community Group Leader?" in this handbook.

Communicate to your apprentice up front that completion of the launch process does not guarantee community group leadership. Often, the launch process will reveal areas of growth that need additional attention. Some of this growth can happen as they lead their new group. Other times, you may need to pause the process in order to work more closely with your apprentice before moving forward. Again, the primary goal is leadership development, not merely starting new groups. Your hub leaders will help you know what steps to take as you move toward multiplication.

5. Launching an Apprentice

At the current group's last gathering, the Smith family sits in the middle of the room as you lead the group in praying for their future as community group leaders. You listen for words, pictures, or passages of Scripture from the Holy Spirit. You also pray for the two other families who are helping launch this new work. Several months later, you invite the Smiths and their community group to rejoin your sending group for a meal. You take turns sharing evidences of God's grace and lead everyone in thanksgiving to God for all that he has done in both groups since the multiplication.

Make an event of your last night together before the multiplication. Throw a party and celebrate what God is doing among you. Put your new community group leaders and their core team in the middle of the room, lay hands on them, and pray for their future together. Mourn the reality of saying goodbye and celebrate God growing his kingdom in your

city through the birth of a new gospel community. Schedule time in the near future to gather back up, share stories of God's grace, and enjoy spending time together again. For more information on multiplication—including how to talk about it and how to plan for it—see the section entitled "Multiplication" in this handbook.

MULTIPLICATION

WHY DO WE MULTIPLY COMMUNITY GROUPS?

Frontline exists to multiply gospel communities that love God, love people, and push back darkness. Through multiplication, we are able to better make disciples, care for others, and advance the kingdom. We multiply so that we can proclaim the gospel and demonstrate the kingdom to more people who desperately need it.

We don't aim to multiply as an end in itself. In other words, our goal is not to launch as many groups as possible. Rather, our community groups multiply for discipleship, care, and mission. If we are to form and sustain healthy groups, multiplication will play a crucial and necessary role.

Multiplication is a very big deal in itself, but what we multiply really matters too. As you prepare for multiplication, do some soul-searching and ask yourself if your community group is faithfully committed to our vision, goals, rhythms, and, ultimately, the gospel. Talk with your hub leader about how you can point your group back towards health as needed.

We multiply for discipleship. When disciples are making disciples, they grow. When community groups increase in number beyond a certain threshold, participation and growth begins to waver because human relationships are inherently limited. We can't know everyone. Leaders can't be everywhere for everyone. Conversations can begin to center around the most vocal people in the group. As a result, mission shrinks, and discipleship is stifled. But through multiplication, we can create room for deeper discipleship and greater intentionality. Multiplication can and should be a means of helping us grow as disciples. We multiply so discipleship can thrive.

We multiply for care. Community groups are responsible for much of the care at Frontline;

therefore, it is crucial to be sensitive to group size and its impact on how we care for one another. When groups grow too large, people can begin to fall through the cracks. Needs might go unknown and unmet. We can easily become overwhelmed and exhausted. The ability to effectively care for one another becomes restricted. But through multiplication, we can keep groups to a reasonable size so that we may know and care for every member. We multiply so care can thrive.

We multiply for mission. Jesus commissioned us to go, and the Church has been committed to multiplication since its inception. We ourselves are recipients of the gospel because Christians throughout history have multiplied and spread the gospel message throughout the world. In the same way, community groups should be reaching out in order to welcome in. We should regularly see new people join our group—both from our church and through relationships in the community. If we are hospitably creating space for others to join us, it will naturally lead to multiplication. When we are on mission, our groups have the potential to grow. When a group is too large, visitors can feel overwhelmed, neglected, and even go unnoticed. We multiply so that mission can thrive and more people can come to know and love Jesus.

HOW DOES SIZE FACTOR INTO MULTIPLICATION?

The size of our groups must be taken into account when thinking about multiplication. The ideal size of a community group is about twelve to eighteen adults. If there are lots of young children in a group, that number might be less. There are exceptions to the rule, but overly-large groups are not our desire and are not usually the best environment for effective discipleship, care, and mission.

When a group is too small, it could turn inward and become less effective at mission. On the other hand, when a group is too large, people might struggle to know and be known in community. The larger the group, the harder it is to shepherd well. It becomes more difficult for everyone to be heard; it becomes harder for everyone to remain organized and accountable. Multiplication should be the objective of a large group sooner rather than later.

WHEN SHOULDN'T YOU MULTIPLY?

Don't multiply just because your group is large.
Group size should not be the primary determining factor for when a group multiplies. While size is incredibly important, what matters most is leader health and readiness. If your group is currently larger than the ideal, we definitely recommend you start having conversations about multiplication. But don't let your group's size dynamics dictate what is wise or rush you into an unhealthy situation.

Don't multiply without trained and qualified leaders.
Before any community group multiplies, we should aim to have leaders who have been trained and equipped to lead a healthy community group. We should avoid rushing someone into leadership so that we can multiply faster. We can't create a shortcut to healthy leadership. If you feel the need to multiply and don't have leaders in mind, talk to your hub leader about ways to develop the right leaders.

Don't multiply to solve relational problems.
Conflict is inevitable in relationships. As we live in community with one another, there will be times we might experience tension, frustration, and anger. We should never use multiplication as an antidote to conflict. Instead, we should encourage healthy, gospel-centered conflict resolution. If a problem persists, contact your hub leader for the best way to move forward.

Don't multiply without a clear sense of mission.
If our reason for multiplying has more to do with convenience than the kingdom, it's just not a good enough reason to multiply. This kind of multiplication is often driven around the felt needs of the group members. *We need to multiply because Thursday nights aren't convenient for me...*

We need to multiply because I don't "click" with Susan... We need to multiply to alleviate _____. Whatever the reason, this is more like division than multiplication, and often reveals a consumeristic heart. The appropriate response is not to multiply, but to patiently lead your group to live in line with the gospel over time (Gal 2:14).

HOW DO I LEAD MY COMMUNITY GROUP THROUGH MULTIPLICATION?

Talk about multiplication from your very first gathering. If a community group is healthy, it will eventually multiply. Set this as an expectation for the community group from the very first gathering and discuss it often. Regularly remind the group members of our missionary identity. Talk about why we multiply, using some of the language found in this section of the handbook. We multiply for discipleship, care, and mission. If you need additional help knowing how to talk to your group about multiplication, talk to your hub leader.

Identify and equip apprentices. You are encouraged to identify and equip apprentices from the start of your group. Every group should have an apprentice as early as possible. For more information on what an apprentice is, and how you can identify and equip them, read the section entitled "Apprenticeship" in this handbook.

Discuss multiplication with your hub leaders. As your group grows and apprentices are developed, contact your hub leader to discuss a potential multiplication. Your hub leaders can help support you, by giving you wisdom on why, when, and how a multiplication should happen. They will also make sure the new group has everything they need for a successful launch.

Talk to your community group about upcoming multiplication. When your community group is ready to move forward with multiplication, it is important to talk to your group about the upcoming plans. A multiplication must be led more than managed. As we share multiplication plans with the group, we have to shepherd as well as communicate. For more details on how to have this conversation, see the section entitled "How Do I Talk To My Community Group About Multiplication?"

Hold a Prayer and Planning Meeting. In prayerful consultation with your hub leaders, and in prayerful collaboration with your apprentices, it is important to make a plan for multiplication. One important step in this process is to hold a Prayer and Planning Meeting with the community group leadership team. For more details on what this step entails, see the section entitled "How Do I Lead a Prayer and Planning Meeting?" in this handbook. Once a new group has a male and female community group leader, a host home, and a core team of at least three households, it is ready to multiply.

Have a sending celebration. On the last gathering before multiplication, throw a party to celebrate the multiplication. Take time to share stories of the things God has done in your midst. Encourage the leaders of the original group and the new group. Prayerfully ask for the Spirit to speak through words or pictures to encourage each group. Take time to pray for the leaders and the groups. It should feel more like a graduation than a funeral. It is also important to recognize that multiplication can be painful, because we have to say goodbye to something good. Still, we can take heart knowing that, through multiplication, more disciples will be made, more people will meet Jesus, and more people will be cared for.

Regather to celebrate. Schedule time in the near future to gather back up, share stories of God's grace, and enjoy spending time together again. It might be ideal to gather a month after multiplication, and then again after six months. Plan a meal or an outdoor party.

HOW DO I TALK TO MY COMMUNITY GROUP ABOUT MULTIPLICATION?

Begin with prayer. Ask for God's grace in the conversation and for each person to remember the unity they have in the Spirit. Pray for God to give wisdom as you discuss the next season of life for the group.

Announce the intention to multiply. Don't drag this step out too long. Let people know that the group is heading towards multiplication, and that you want to take time to process that with the group right now. Avoid seeking total consensus or surveying the group's preferences as a first step. You could say something like "As a leadership team, we feel it is time to move our group towards multiplication."

Talk about the "why" of multiplication. This point will be easier if you have already laid the groundwork for multiplication from the very first gathering (see the section entitled "How Do I Lead My Group Through Multiplication?"). But even if you haven't, you can still shape a vision for multiplication now. In particular, we multiply for discipleship, care, and mission. You can find a paragraph explaining each one of these in the section entitled "Why Do We Multiply Community Groups?" If you need even more tools for explaining this vision, don't hesitate to reach out to your hub leaders.

Let apprentices briefly share. As those who will be leading out a new group, give the apprentices space to share their desires and hopes for leading. Group members should already have a sense for the apprentices' character and competency. This time gives the apprentices an opportunity to express their own sense of calling. This shouldn't last longer than five minutes, and could be as short as a couple sentences. For example, they could say, "When the community group leaders approached us a few months ago about leading a new group, we weren't so sure. But as we've prayed about it and learned more about leadership, we feel God moving us in that direction. And we are really excited about getting a chance to serve in this way."

Outline next steps for the group. Give the community group a roadmap for what the next steps will look like. Let them know you plan to do the following: (1) Schedule an upcoming Prayer and Planning Meeting where the leaders and apprentices will pray and draw up a multiplication plan. (2) Extend to each member a personal invitation into one of the groups, coming out of that meeting (from either a leader or an apprentice). (3) Give each person time to prayerfully consider and give feedback. (4) Schedule a sending celebration for the last gathering before the multiplication takes place.

Calm fears and anxieties. You can do this as you outline the next steps for the group, or give it its own section. First, explain that this process will be done prayerfully and with a desire to serve each person's spiritual growth. Second, it is important to stress that if anyone does not want to join the group into which they are invited, they are welcome to join the other group instead. By honoring the group members in this way, leaders can avoid the ditch of controlling leadership on the one hand, and passive leadership on the other. Most people—if they know their leaders have approached the process prayerfully, and not removed their freedom—will gladly accept whichever invitation is extended to them. Also, keep in mind that many fears and anxieties will be brought up after this initial announcement outside of a gathering. Be prepared to address concerns over the next few weeks in organic, one-on-one conversations.

Give members space to voice concerns or questions. Give everyone space to share what they are feeling or thinking. Don't feel pressure to argue or refute what people are saying. Instead, listen humbly, take note, and thank them for sharing. Also, don't be discouraged or surprised by negativity. People are not always as resistant as they sound initially. Sometimes, the process of sharing concerns is part of getting their head around the idea, especially if multiplication hasn't been talked about much up to this point.

HOW DO I LEAD A PRAYER AND PLANNING MEETING?

There are many ways to multiply a group, and there are many tensions to navigate in the process. A Prayer and Planning Meeting is one simple strategy that has been proven to help group leaders tiptoe through the landmines. A community group's leaders and apprentices constitute a leadership team or "core team." This leadership team should set up a group phone call or in-person meeting to pray for and plan the multiplication. If they need additional help, they can invite one or both of their hub leaders—or even their community director—to sit in on the call or in-person meeting.

The primary goal of this meeting is to prayerfully and pastorally guide the members of the current group into two viable future groups. The current leaders can plan to lead one of the groups, and the apprentices the other. At the very beginning of the

meeting, the leadership team should spend time praying, asking for the unity of the Spirit throughout the planning meeting (Eph 4:3). Further, they should pray for the Spirit's guidance and wisdom as they plan. God hears our prayers and gives us wisdom when we need it. And without God's grace and direction, multiplication can devolve into a messy, divisive, and hurtful process.

Throughout the meeting, the leadership team should remind each other that the goal is to look primarily through the lens of what will serve each person's spiritual growth. All things being equal, the multiplication plan should preserve or increase, rather than diminish, the following:

- intergenerational diversity
- geographical proximity
- a balance of single and married
- a balance of low and high margin
- a balance of spiritual maturity and immaturity

Every group member will have personal preferences, or a particular comfort level with every other person in the group. Those factors should not be ignored, but they are secondary. Multiplication must first be governed by the mission of God, not the anxiety of any given member.

Sometimes the current discipleship groups—if they have been constructed thoughtfully—will draw the lines for the multiplication, with almost no alteration needed. Other times, the leadership team will need to wrestle with the tensions listed above. Regardless, each member of the leadership team must be prepared to embrace discomfort and prayerfully set aside their own preferences.

In the Prayer and Planning Meeting, leaders and apprentices should seek to contribute to the overall health of the process. Here are some examples of what might be said:

- "Sarah was invited to the group by you, Nancy, and you have built a lot of trust with her over the past six months. We're not quite sure where Sarah is with Jesus yet, and it seems like it would be wise for Sarah to be in the same group as you, so you can continue to capitalize on the trust you've built with her."

- "I know Robert wears on people, and can lack self-awareness, but for some reason God's given me a lot of patience for him. He is learning, even though it's a slow process. I would like him in both my community group and my discipleship group. I really think I can serve him in some unique ways as he continues to grow."

- "Hey, let's make sure we don't end up putting all the married couples in one group and all the singles in the other."

- "We have a few people who live in the Miller Neighborhood. It would be great to plant a gospel flag in that neighborhood. If one of the groups could be hosted in that neighborhood, it could provide some great opportunities to build relationships with people far from God."

Designate a secretary to write down the names for the proposed new groups. After the meeting, to ensure clarity, the secretary should text or email the names to the other leaders and apprentices.

At the conclusion of the meeting, the leaders and apprentices should commit to the plan. Humble disagreement in the meeting, behind closed doors, is an important part of the decision-making process. However, once the plan is drawn up and agreed on, it is crucial that the leadership team stay on the same page moving forward. If a leader or apprentice has second thoughts after leaving the meeting, it will be important for them to circle back with the leadership team and reopen the conversation, and then come to a new agreement.

After the Prayer and Planning Meeting, the leaders and apprentices should personally invite each person into their respective groups, while giving them space to provide feedback or voice their desire to be a part of the other group. This step is important because sometimes group members will see something the leaders have missed about geographical proximity, missional possibility, or relational opportunity. The leadership team should communicate frequently with each other about how these conversations are going, and pass on any insights group members provide.

HOW DO WE PREPARE FOR THE LOSS OF MULTIPLICATION?

We have to acknowledge that multiplication will be accompanied by pain and loss. And we must not minimize that. It will be hard for people to let go of something good and real, even if it is for the right reasons. The sense of loss we experience around multiplication should not only be acknowledged, but in a real sense, embraced. It will be very difficult to celebrate multiplication unless we feel and experience the pain of gospel goodbyes.

Through multiplication, many of us will feel instability as the ground shifts beneath us. For those who have never experienced a multiplication, it will be normal to feel fear about the unknown and what losses might come through this. On the other hand, for those who have already been through a multiplication, it will be normal to feel multiplication fatigue and wonder if they will ever have stability. For both groups of people, it will be important to acknowledge fear, while also recognizing what Jesus is doing in us and for us through multiplication.

In multiplication, we often have to say goodbye to something good. Relationships might look different as we establish new rhythms and enter a new season. The pain of loss points to the reality that we experienced something beautiful. But we can recognize it as a gospel goodbye, because we have hope that transcends our grief—that Jesus will use this for his glory and our joy.

Every group multiplication leads to gospel goodbyes. Gospel goodbyes can be tearful and sad, yet they are ultimately tinged with hope and joy. We can even find ourselves celebrating in the midst of loss because we know that we are making room for more people to be discipled, to receive care, and to meet Jesus. Even as our relationships change, we can rejoice that we are still united together in Jesus by the Spirit.

COMMUNITY GROUP LEADER FAQ

HOW DO I FILL OUT THE WEEKLY REPORT?

Community group leaders fill out a weekly report to take attendance, record notes, and pass along any prayer requests or important information. These reports are confidential and only seen by the community director and hub leaders. In weekly reports, a group leader can notify the leaders of the church about important seasons of care, like marriage, pregnancy, miscarriage, suffering, etc.

Every week, you will receive an email called "Weekly Report." Work through the following steps:

• *"Record Attendance" or "Did Not Meet" buttons:* If you are meeting as a whole group, click "Record Attendance." If the group is not meeting or is meeting in discipleship groups, click, "Did Not Meet," and in the "Event Notes" section just write either "did not meet" or "discipleship group." Give any updates that may be helpful.

• *Recording your attendance:* After clicking "Record Attendance" your community group roster will appear. Take attendance at your group. Then go through and check the names of those present. In the "Visitors" section, put the number of those present whose names were not in your roster and you therefore did not check. For example, if you had fourteen people present, and you checked twelve names, type "two" in the "Visitors" space so the total will be correct. If you would like people added to or deleted from your list, please use the "People Info" space to request it. If you would prefer to manage your own roster and group through CCB (our database), email your hub leader and request a CCB login.

• *Info spaces:* In the "Event Notes" space, please provide a sentence explanation of what your group did that night.

In the "Praises and Prayer Requests" space, please share encouraging stories and let us know of anything you would like for us to be praying for.

This is the correct place to let the pastors know if someone is going through a season of care.

In the "People Info" space, please tell us if you would like for us to add or delete anyone from your roster. If asking to delete someone, please let us know the circumstances. Feel free to use this space to let us know life updates on your members as well.

• *Email event summary:* Finally, you are asked where to send the report summary. Select, "Leadership Only". If you do not select this button, your hub leader will not receive your report.

HOW DO I HANDLE THE SUMMER AND WINTER BREAKS?

God has created our world and our bodies with rhythmic cycles of work and rest. Community groups take two breaks throughout the year: one in July and one in December. These are natural moments where people are scattered on vacations or celebrations, and they present a healthy opportunity for leaders to take a break from regular leadership duties. Here are three things you can do during the break to make the best use of the time.

• *Communicate expectations to your community group.* The summer and winter break should serve as a "leadership sabbatical." Push pause on your group leadership duties for that month. As you do so, let people in the group know that you will be using the month to rest and recover. Make clear any boundaries you are wanting to set during the break.

• *Establish a Sabbath rhythm.* We are not resting well if we simply replace the work of leading a community group with other work. We should use the time to establish healthy Sabbath rhythms. Consider reading the chapter entitled "Practice Sabbath Delight," in Peter Scazzaro's *The Emotionally Healthy Leader* to help you answer practical questions like: What will make this Sabbath day different from business as usual on the other six days of the week? What do I need to do to protect my ability to rest on this day?

- **Take a personal inventory.** Take some time over the course of the break to assess your life and leadership. Where would you like to grow? Where have you seen God's grace? What do you hope to accomplish in your community group in the next six months? Taking a break can give you space to process these questions and maximize your health when you step back into leadership. If it helps you, consider taking the "Reality Check Self-Assessment" to determine if there are any warning lights popping up on your dashboard (*frontlinechurch.com/library*).

Just like taking a weekly sabbath requires preparation in the days leading up to it, you'll need to work diligently before the break in order to truly unplug. Here are four things you could do.

1. **Schedule your restart.** Before the break, communicate clearly a hard restart date for your community group. For example, "Our group will resume our family meals on Tuesday, August 6th at 6:30pm at the Johnsons. Please mark your calendars and bring meat to grill and a side to share."

2. **Encourage group members to pair up relationally.** These should be very informal, gender-specific pairings, doing something as big as a meal, or something as small as a walk around the lake. This allows relationships to grow and deepen, and reminds everyone to keep pressing into communion during the break.

3. **Commission others to throw a summer or winter party.** Ask your community group members to plan and host a party for the group during the break. This allows people in the group to take ownership, and provides a connection point during the break.

4. **If applicable, set a multiplication plan in place.** The summer and winter breaks are an ideal time for community groups to multiply. Getting all the logistics and pastoral concerns nailed down prior to the break will make multiplication flow much more smoothly afterwards.

If a care need arises during the summer or winter break, communicate with your hub leader on the best way to move forward and respond.

HOW DO I HANDLE CARE SITUATIONS IN MY COMMUNITY GROUP?

We begin to care in community by simply being open with each other about our own needs. Then, with a loving and thoughtful disposition, we respond collectively to meet those needs. This means regularly sharing where we are and what we are wrestling with, and being courageous enough to ask for and accept help. When we respond collectively and quickly to real needs as they arise, people are loved and cared for. Sometimes more specific, intentional care is required. When this is the case, you will need to gather information and determine what level of care is needed. In general, there are two levels of formal care:

- **Community Group Driven Care:** If the care situation is not an emergency and does not require immediate attention, your community group should drive care, while communicating with your hub leadership team via weekly reports. You should follow up with the individual receiving care as needed, but, in general, you should be touching base with them at least once a month. Examples might include pregnancies, weddings, or minor illnesses.

- **Hub Leader or Elder Driven Care:** If you determine that no one in the group is equipped to handle the need or if the need requires immediate, pastoral, or professional care, contact your hub leaders immediately. From there, hub leadership or other elders will drive care if necessary, while maintaining frequent communication with your community group. Examples might include divorce, criminal behavior, miscarriages, major mental health issues, or death. In some cases, these individuals may be referred to outside professionals, like counselors, mental health professionals, DHS, or the police.

If you ever feel overwhelmed, have a question on who should drive care, or are unsure how to care for an individual in a care situation, contact your hub leaders and ask for help.

WHEN SHOULD I ELEVATE A CARE ISSUE TO MY HUB LEADERS?

Though a good deal of care will be provided by your community group, there are some things that you simply will not be able to handle, and, if left unattended, could lead to major physical, emotional, or spiritual harm for the individuals on the receiving end of our care. These are typically situations that require the help of deacons, elders, or outside professionals. With that in mind, if you encounter any of the following situations, you should contact a hub leader immediately.

- Marital or family problems
- Adultery
- Marital separation or divorce
- Hospital admission or surgery
- Miscarriage
- Death
- Mental health issues
- Psychotic episode
- Suicidal behavior
- Addictions
- Financial problems or benevolence needs
- Unemployment
- Legal issues
- Unrepentant sin patterns
- Egregious sin
- Predatory behavior
- Physical or sexual abuse
- Criminal behavior
- Chronic absence from the church or community group
- Major disagreements with the church
- Crisis of faith
- Leaving the church

Again, if you ever feel overwhelmed, have a question on who should drive care, or are unsure how to care for an individual in a care situation, contact your hub leaders and ask for help.

WHAT DO I DO IN EMERGENCY SITUATIONS?

If a group member or child is in immediate danger or has been the victim of domestic violence or abuse, call 911.

If a group member is experiencing a mental health crisis, call the Suicide & Crisis Lifeline at 988.

(According to the Suicide & Crisis Lifeline, a mental health crisis is any situation in which a person's actions, feelings, and behaviors can lead to them hurting themselves or others, and/or put them at risk of being unable to care for themselves or function in the community in a healthy manner.)

If you have witnessed abuse of a child, an adult with disabilities, or an elderly person, or if you suspect that it may have occurred or that there is potential for abuse to occur, call the Statewide Abuse and Neglect Hotline at 1-800-522-3511. You have a legal obligation under state law to promptly report current or potential instances of abuse.

After contacting the appropriate authorities, when it is safe to do so, contact your hub leaders and fill them in on the situation.

WHERE CAN I GET RESOURCES ON SPECIFIC CARE SITUATIONS?

If you are needing help knowing how to care for community group members who are dealing with specific issues (such as depression, addiction, finances, or pornograpy), reach out to your hub leader who can give you resources, as well as guidance on particular issues.

WHAT IF SOMEONE IS DRAINING THE GROUP?

How you handle this situation depends on the particular person in question. If the individual simply lacks social skills, or is behaving in a socially inappropriate manner, it is important to help them by having a private conversation with them to lovingly address the behaviors that are disrupting the group. However, more often than not, those who drain the group do not do so intentionally. In fact, very often the draining behavior stems from legitimate suffering or struggle and only becomes draining when the individual begins to expect their group to meet their needs in ways only God can. It is important to remember that we have all been the draining person to someone else at some point.

In some unavoidable ways, suffering turns us inward. Counterintuitively, the answer is often to simply move towards the draining person. As we encourage each other to look to Christ in the midst of our suffering, we are helped and reoriented. One of the best ways to address draining behavior within the group is to pursue that person outside of the group.

This is a perfect opportunity for an apprentice to gain valuable experience. As the apprentice invites that person to coffee, hears their story, and prays for them, they will grow in skill and wisdom. And hopefully, the draining person will begin to find their footing as they are counseled and met in the midst of their sin, wounds, and weakness.

Remember, you are not and cannot be anyone's savior. Once you and your group realize this and rest in God's sovereign purpose, the person in question will become less of a drain. Some individuals need specialized care, so you may also suggest biblical counseling. Contact a hub leader for counseling references.

A FINAL WORD ON COMMUNITY GROUP LEADERSHIP

When you encounter problems, the worst thing you can do is to ignore them and hope they will go away. It is unlikely that they will disappear without being addressed. If you let them go on unchecked, the members of the group will gradually cease to attend as their dissatisfaction with the group grows. Your failure to act could lead to the death of the group. Remember, your chief job as a leader is to do everything in your power to point people to Jesus and lead the group to function as a healthy community. This will occasionally require you doing things that don't come naturally, and even seem unpleasant. But love for God's people and concern for their wellbeing ought to serve as sufficient motivation for carrying out these difficult tasks.

PART 3

DISCIPLESHIP GROUPS

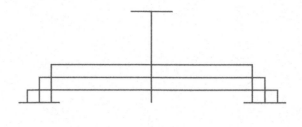

People do not drift toward holiness. Apart from grace-driven effort, people do not gravitate toward godliness, prayer, obedience to Scripture, faith, and delight in the Lord. We drift toward compromise and call it tolerance; we drift toward disobedience and call it freedom; we drift toward superstition and call it faith. We cherish the indiscipline of lost self-control and call it relaxation; we slouch toward prayerlessness and delude ourselves into thinking we have escaped legalism; we slide toward godlessness and convince ourselves we have been liberated.

D. A. CARSON
For the Love of God

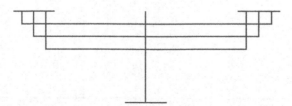

DISCIPLESHIP GROUPS

Gender-specific groups of three or four who gather regularly to know and encourage one another in their walk with Jesus

WHAT IS A DISCIPLESHIP GROUP?

If community doesn't draw us deeper into discipleship, it will become just another way to hide in plain sight. A discipleship group is ideally formed from within a community group, though there are some exceptions to this. As we grow in trust and safety with one another, we will more effectively be able to disciple one another.

Jonathan Dodson, in his book *Gospel-Centered Discipleship*, warns us about the common pitfalls that discipleship groups may face. Our discipleship groups should be centered around the gospel and avoid the ditches of "religious" and "irreligious" groups. Religious discipleship groups traffic in "cuss jar" accountability, where the members can only offer one another shame and punishment. Instead of trusting by faith that Jesus took our punishment on the cross and atoned for our sin, we try to atone for our sins through what Dodson calls "mutual punishment." As a result, religious discipleship groups tempt people to start lying or stop coming. *Religious discipleship groups don't last long because eventually everyone gets bled to death.*

"Irreligious" discipleship groups traffic in "confession booth" accountability, where we confess our sins and pat each other on the back. We leave feeling better, but with little changed or challenged. Instead of passionately pursuing "the holiness without which no one will see the Lord" (Heb 12:14), irreligious discipleship groups devolve into false peace, where we get things off our chest, but never take steps to grow in obedience. Our confession stops short of repentance as we confess the same sins over and over, but refuse to take violent action against them. *Irreligious discipleship groups don't*

last long because eventually everyone gets bored to death.

On the other hand, in a healthy, gospel-centered discipleship group, we remind each other that while we are more sinful than we dared feared, we are more loved than we dared hope, because of Jesus' death in our place. Together, we confess our sins, we point each other to Jesus, and we encourage each other to live in line with the gospel.

WHAT DOES A DISCIPLESHIP GROUP DO?

When a discipleship group gathers together, it typically includes four movements that help a group become more balanced, biblical, and fruitful.

1. Scripture. Briefly check in on your engagement with Scripture since your last gathering. As David Powlison puts it, what's one bit of Scripture you are applying to one bit of your life? One bit of Scripture can lead you to adore God, see and hate your sin, or ask for grace. To apply one bit of Scripture to one bit of your life requires at least meditation, if not memorization. *This will be the most difficult of the four movements to practice outside of your group, but it will be the single greatest determiner of the quality of what happens in your group.* Consider the sobering reality that many of us do not consistently spend time alone with God—connecting with him through Scripture and prayer.

Out of a misguided fear of being legalistic, many Christians are afraid to exhort each other to grow in connecting with God through the basic, quiet acts of reading Scripture and praying. We should be afraid of legalism (religion), but we should also be *equally* afraid of license (irreligion). Striving to increasingly obey Scripture's clear command to read Scripture and pray only becomes legalistic when it is done as an attempt to earn God's forgiveness or avoid his punishment, rather than as a glad response to having already been forgiven through Jesus. Regularly feeding on Scripture and praying is non-optional for Christians (1 Tim 2:8; Josh 1:8; 2 Tim 3:16—17; Eph 6:18). Where we often go wrong is when we attempt to work *for* God's acceptance rather than working *from* God's acceptance. In the words of Dallas Willard, "Grace is not opposed to effort, it is opposed to earning."

In Colossians 3:16, Paul urges all Christians to "let the word of Christ dwell in you richly, teaching and admonishing one another in all wisdom, singing psalms and hymns and spiritual songs, with thankfulness in your hearts to God." How can we teach and admonish each other with "all wisdom" if the Word of Christ is not dwelling in us richly? It is likely that most members of any given group may not know how to meditate on Scripture or pray in a meaningful way. Even if they do, they are probably doing it no more than one or two days a week. In light of this normative cultural reality, expect to spend the first six to twelve months of a newly-formed discipleship group repeatedly returning to the discipline of spending time alone with God, and patiently, practically equipping each other to read, meditate on, memorize, and pray Scripture.

If multiple of you are repeatedly showing up not having read your Bibles, make a shift in your discipleship group. Instead of continuing to answer the Scripture question in the negative, take 20 minutes at the beginning of your gathering to read Scripture together over the next several weeks. You can use the alternate Discipleship Group Guide, which outlines how to have a discipleship group in this way. You can find this guide later in this section of this handbook or online at *frontlinechurch.com/ discipleship*.

2. Sharing. Briefly check in personally. How is God changing you for the good (sanctification)? What are you facing that's hard (suffering)? What sin or temptation do you need to confess (sin)? David Powlison points out that covering each of these areas allows us to look at the whole picture. This approach is informed by Scripture and is full of love and compassion, while at the same time preventing imbalance in several directions. In other words, some groups dive deep into confession of sin, but neglect to encourage each other by pointing out growth they see in each other—however small. Other groups dive deep into what's hard, but neglect honest and specific confession of sin.

In his book *Side by Side*, Ed Welch points out that many of us don't even know how to talk about sin with others. When someone confesses sin, we shouldn't simply commiserate. Instead, we should aim for the heart, work to develop a plan, and recognize the messy nature of growth and change. We should always consider which of us might be particularly vulnerable in the present moment (traveling, suffering, loneliness, etc.). We should feel concerned if we can't identify our own temptations, and blessed if we can. For all of us, our goal should be to bring our sins out into the open and grow in saying "no" to sinful desires (Titus 2:11-12). And in every situation, we should thank God for any good fruit we can spot.

3. Spread of the Gospel. Remind the group of the names of your "three," and briefly check-in. How is it going pursuing and praying for them? Your goal should be to prayerfully name three people who don't follow Jesus within your sphere of influence. You will then commit to pray for and engage them in intentional gospel relationships. These people could be your children, family, friends, co-workers, neighbors, or others. Whom would you most love to see become a disciple of Jesus? Who is your heart best shaped to reach for Jesus? Alan Hirsch suggests that we continually ask: (1) Are we in close proximity with those we feel called to? (2) Are we spending regular time with these people? (3) Are we too busy to develop meaningful relationships?

Naming and praying for your "three" every time you gather will guard your group against spiritual navel-gazing and self-obsession. If you haven't identified your three, use this time to write down your three, and then pray together, right on the spot, for God to give you the opportunity to: (1) build a deeper relationship with them, (2) introduce them to Christian community, and (3) share the gospel with them. Pray together that God would save them by opening their eyes to the beauty of Jesus (2 Cor 4:6).

4. *Spirit-Filled Prayer.* After someone has shared, respond with Spirit-filled prayer. Make sure that your gatherings don't descend into Christianized "talk therapy." In mutual discipleship, sharing that does not pivot to prayer is quickly headed toward self-effort fueled by self-will. No one changes apart from the transforming power of the Spirit. Consider three common barriers to prayer. First, *presumption.* It has been well said that we should not presume that God will do for us apart from prayer what he has explicitly promised to do for us only through prayer! Second, *unbelief.* In the words of an old British missions pamphlet, if our prayer is meager it is because we regard it as supplemental rather than fundamental. Third, *boredom.* Often we don't pray because, if we're honest, we find prayer boring. *This will be the most difficult of the four movements to practice in the group, but it will be the single greatest determiner of the quality of what happens outside of the group.*

How do you create an effective, God-glorifying, life-transforming discipleship group? In the words of Ed Welch, pray one minute longer than you talk! Far too often, when Christians gather, prayer is tacked on at the end and rushed through hurriedly in five minutes or less, after the "real work" of talk therapy and unasked for advice-giving has dragged on for hours. Strive to put heart-centered, Spirit-filled, Scripture-infused prayer at the center, and you will never leave a gathering with a sense of having wasted your time.

Possible signs we are inviting the Spirit into our prayers: (1) when our prayers comfortably move in and out of silence, (2) when we find ourselves praying more than once, and (3) when we pray Scripture, thoughts, pictures, and even gut impressions, spontaneously brought to mind by God. We should always filter these impressions through Scripture, as well as weigh and test them in wise community (1 Thess 5:21; 1 Cor 14:29). We should pray, not only for God to change our circumstances when they are hard, but also to meet us in the midst of those circumstances, to change our hearts and allow us to bear fruit. We can even take the Lord's Prayer line by line, allowing it to direct our prayers towards thanksgiving, confession, requests, and worship.

A guide outlining a discipleship group gathering can be found on the next two pages (download a PDF at *frontlinechurch.com/discipleship*).

Important: Before your first meeting, everyone should listen to the 45 minute teaching found at *frontlinechurch.com/aimfortheheart*.

Instructions

1. Invite someone to share.
2. Set a timer for 15 minutes.
3. Have them answer the five questions below.
4. When the timer goes off, take 5 minutes to pray for that person, and for their three.

▸ Repeat until everyone has shared and received prayer.
▸ Groups of three should set aside at least an hour, and groups of four at least an hour and a half.

Scripture

Briefly check in on your engagement with Scripture since meeting together last.

1. What's one bit of Scripture you're applying to one bit of your life?

Sharing

Briefly check in personally.

2. How's God changing you for the good (sanctification)?
   What can we celebrate with you?

3. What are you facing that's hard (suffering)?
   How can we sympathize with you?

4. What sin or temptation do you need to confess (sin)?
   How can we pray for you and help you?

Spread of the Gospel

Remind the group of the names of your three, and briefly check-in.

5. How's it going pursuing and praying for your three?

Spirit-Filled Prayer

After someone has shared, respond with Spirit-filled prayer.

Tip: *Establish relationship first.* Before diving into this guide, it is important to establish the kind of relational connection that will invite more personal sharing. Start by sharing life stories—perhaps one or two per meeting. This concise guide will help each of you prepare to share: *frontlinechurch.com/lifestories*.

Tip: *If you are repeatedly showing up not having read your Bibles, switch to using the other side of this sheet for your next eight meetings.* Instead of continuing to answer Question 1 below in the negative, you'll take the first 20 minutes of each meeting to read and apply a passage of Scripture together, on the spot.

Tip: *Don't be afraid to pivot to prayer when the timer goes off.* Do your meetings keep going long? Are you failing to make time for everyone to share? Sharing is important, but prayer provides the power to change! Sometimes when a person needs additional time to share, that's simply a sign that you should set up additional time to meet and pray with them outside of your regular meetings.

One bit of Scripture can do any number of things. It can lead you to (1) adore God, (2) see and hate your sin, or (3) ask for grace. To apply one bit of Scripture to one bit of your life requires at least meditation if not memorization. For more: *bit.ly/bitofscript*.

When someone confesses sin, we shouldn't simply commiserate. Instead, we should aim for the heart, work to develop a plan, and recognize the messy nature of growth and change. We should feel concerned if we can't identify our own temptations, and blessed if we can. Our chief goal? Bring our sins out into the open and grow in saying no to restless desires (Titus 2:11–12). For more: *bit.ly/talkaboutsin*.

Who are your "three"? Prayerfully name three people who don't follow Jesus within your sphere of influence. You will then commit to pray for and engage them in intentional gospel relationships. These people could be your children, family, friends, co-workers, neighbors, or others. Whom would you most love to see become a disciple of Jesus? Who is your heart best shaped to reach for Jesus? Naming and praying for your three every time you gather will guard your group against spiritual navel-gazing and self-obsession.

Possible signs we are inviting the Spirit into our prayers: (1) when our prayers comfortably move in and out of silence, (2) when we find ourselves praying more than once, and (3) when we pray Scripture, thoughts, pictures, and even gut impressions, spontaneously brought to mind by God—filtering them by Scripture and weighing them in wise community. See: *bit.ly/spiritfilledpraying*.

Alternate Instructions

1. Pick one of the six reading plans, and spend 20 minutes working through the directions listed under "Scripture" below.

....

Then shift to working through the questions.
2. Invite someone to share.
3. Set a timer for 10 minutes.
4. Have them answer the five questions below.
5. When the timer goes off, take 5 minutes to pray for that person, and for their three.

....

‣ Repeat until everyone has shared and received prayer.
‣ Groups of three should set aside at least one hour, and groups of four at least an hour and a half.

#	✔	Mark	Colossians	Romans	Genesis	Psalms	Micah
1	☐	1:1–15	1:1–14	5:1–11	1:1–2:3	1	1–2
2	☐	2:1–12	1:15–23	5:12–21	2:4–25	2	3
3	☐	3:7–35	1:24–2:5	6:1–14	3	42	4
4	☐	8:22–38	2:6–23	6:15–23	4–5	73	5:1–6
5	☐	10:17–45	3:1–4	7:1–6	6–7	90	5:7–15
6	☐	14:53–15:15	3:5–17	7:7–25	8–9	91	6:1–8
7	☐	15:16–39	3:18–4:1	8:1–17	11	107	6:9–16
8	☐	15:42–16:8	4:2–18	8:18–39	12	121	7:1–20

Scripture

....

‣ Briefly pray and ask God to open your eyes to see wonderful things in his Word (Ps 119:18).

‣ Then read the passage out loud together.

‣ Take 10 minutes to read back over the passage on your own, and look for three things: a **star**, a **question mark**, and an **arrow** (see descriptions in sidebar).

‣ As you read on your own, try to write down one to three things under each category.

‣ Talk about what you wrote down with your group.
- Each share a star, and discuss.
- Each share a question mark, and then do your best to work out answers together from the passage. Don't feel pressure to come up with an answer for every question right now. *Don't get bogged down here!*
- Each share an arrow, and discuss.

 A star: anything that shines out in the passage and draws attention—it can be something important, or something that strikes you

....

 A question mark: anything that is hard to understand—something that you would like to be able to ask the author about

....

 An arrow: anything that applies personally to your everyday life

....

One-to-One Bible Reading: A Simple Guide for Every Christian, David Helm

---

Sharing

Briefly check in personally.

1. How's God changing you for the good (sanctification)? *What can we celebrate with you?*

2. What are you facing that's hard (suffering)? *How can we sympathize with you?*

3. What sin or temptation do you need to confess (sin)? *How can we pray for you and help you?*

Spread of the Gospel

Remind the group of the names of your three, and briefly check-in.

4. How's it going pursuing and praying for your three?

Spirit-Filled Prayer

After someone has shared, respond with Spirit-filled prayer.

DISCIPLESHIP GROUPS FAQ

HOW DO I START A DISCIPLESHIP GROUP?

If your community group doesn't have any discipleship groups, take steps to form them during family meal. Taking the members of a community group and helping them form into smaller discipleship groups can feel fuzzy—maybe even a bit overwhelming or risky. But as community groups grow in age, they should grow in relational depth, with the hope that these relationships could grow into discipleship groups. One step you can take is to use the family meal as an opportunity to practice discipleship groups. Either during or after the meal, separate the men and women to share more deeply. It might look like saying, "All the men are going into the kitchen, and the women are going into the den. Talk about what's been going on in your life, and pray for one another." Maybe do this every other time you meet. After you do this a few times, people will begin to feel more comfortable being vulnerable around one another, and potential leaders will emerge. You now have the seeds to start multiple potential discipleship groups.

Identify facilitators. Discipleship groups work best when someone takes on the responsibility to facilitate the group. Facilitators help drive communication, and keep the gatherings focused. Look for the leaders that naturally emerge during your normal gatherings—people who are particularly good at listening to others. People who know how to aim for the heart and move conversations deeper. People who are humble, gentle, patient, and loving (Eph 4:2). They've experienced how God's kindness leads us to repentance, so they avoid using guilt and shame to manage other people's stuck patterns of sin. On the other hand, they've also experienced how the same grace that saves us, changes us, so neither do they excuse other people's sin. They have a gospel confidence about them that comes out in the calm and thoughtful way they listen, encourage, and walk alongside others who are stuck or hurting.

They don't panic when people around them are sinning and suffering. These are people who will at the least do no harm, and who will at the most do a great deal of good. People who live like this are going to emerge in those potential discipleship groups mentioned in the previous point. Once you have identified facilitators, invite them to serve in this role and participate in a Prayer and Planning Meeting to create discipleship groups.

Follow the sections entitled "How Do I Talk To My Community Group About Multiplication?" and "How Do I Lead a Prayer and Planning Meeting?" under the "Multiplication" section of this handbook. These sections outline how to plan and communicate a community group multiplication, but the same principles generally apply to starting discipleship groups. Talk to your community group about the importance of discipleship groups. Have a Prayer and Planning Meeting with the community group leaders and prospective facilitators. Out of these steps, create discipleship groups of three or four people, including a facilitator over each.

Encourage everyone to do a little homework before they start. Before you gather for the first time, the discipleship group facilitator should listen to the audio training on how to facilitate a gospel-centered discipleship group (*frontlinechurch.com/discipleship*). In addition, everyone in the discipleship group should set aside time to listen to the audio teaching on the do's and don'ts of discipleship groups, entitled "When in Doubt, Aim for the Heart" (*frontlinechurch.com/aimfortheheart*). When you gather for the first time, discuss how you were each personally instructed or corrected by that teaching. These trainings can be found at *frontlinechurch.com/discipleship*.

Establish confidentiality. Once a new group is formed, discuss confidentiality at the outset. Give each person in the room the opportunity to describe how they understand the mutual commitment they're making to confidentiality. Decide what you will share or not share with your spouses, if any of you are married. It is important that you not repeat anything that was shared with you in confidence in the context of a discipleship group unless you (1) get permission from the person, or (2) believe there is some potentially harmful or criminal act being perpetrated against them or others, or (3) determine someone is consistently defiant and unrepentant in their sin.

Share life stories. When you first begin to gather as a discipleship group, dedicate time to sharing your stories. Don't rush through this step. As we know each other more deeply and understand where we have been in our life, we will be able to better disciple one another towards Jesus. It might take several meetings for you to allow everyone to share their story. For more information on how to share your story, see the section entitled "How Do We Share Our Life Stories?"

Lead by facilitation. Leadership in a discipleship group is by facilitation, meaning, the leader is a peer who is merely helping to keep conversation moving and focused. The facilitator should never feel more important than the others, or that they need to present a false spirituality. Rather, they should lead by example in recognizing their need and in being vulnerable. Facilitators should regularly communicate any needs or concerns with their community group leaders.

Strive for consistency and clarity. Our goal is that discipleship groups would meet at least twice a month, typically on the second and fourth week of the month. Yet we should recognize that on occasion, people will not be able to come. When you launch a new discipleship group, make it a priority to be there whenever possible. Put it in your calendar. As much as is realistically possible, try and meet on the same day at the same time in the same place. By meeting regularly, we not only maintain relationship, but we can also grow in vulnerability and depth. Avoid canceling. If at least one other person can attend, the facilitator should still meet with them. As we model consistency, we teach our people what they should value and imitate.

When you meet, use the Discipleship Group Guide. After the first few gatherings where you share your stories, use the Discipleship Group Guide as a template for your time together. This guide allows everyone to share and prevents anyone from dominating the conversation. You can refer to the guide earlier in this section, or print off physical copies at *frontlinechurch.com/discipleship*.

HOW DO WE SHARE OUR LIFE STORIES?

Planning to Share. Identify who will share their story ahead of time. In other words, as a rule, don't ask people to share right on the spot. To tell their story well, people need time to reflect and pray. If you're the one who has been asked to share next, consider writing your story down to help you reflect and share. You may even need to simply read what you have written when your turn comes. Sharing your story may take up to 30 minutes.

If you have a story you have never told anyone—or told very few people—and you are wrestling with what to share or how to share it in a way that will protect you and edify others, reach out to one (or several) of your leaders and ask if you can process your story with them in private ahead of time. That way, when you share your story, it will be the second time you share, and it will also allow you, with the help of your leaders, to discern what to share or not share and how best to share it.

Preparing to Share. As we prepare to tell our stories, it's best to examine and talk about our lives in three ways: (1) how we have grown, (2) how we have suffered, and (3) how we have sinned. It's easy to fall into a "just the facts" format when sharing our life stories, but if we think of our stories as just a list of dates, places, and names, we won't end up sharing the parts of our story that are most meaningful and that help others begin to really know us. Instead, we should think about how we would answer the following questions: *How has God used the good, bad, and really difficult things in my life to form me into the person I am today? Who was I before I met Jesus? How has Jesus changed me? Who am I becoming?*

Prayerfully Responding When We Share. After someone has shared, be sure to immediately and vocally thank the person who shared their story and affirm their courage and vulnerability, especially if it was a hard or painful story to share. If it moved you, blessed you, or broke your heart, respond and say those things out loud to that person.

Finally, gather around the person who has shared and pray for them. Have multiple people lay hands on them—asking their permission first, if that is a new experience for them or if they are particularly emotional. Pray vocal and compassionate prayers over them, inviting the Holy Spirit to minister to them in that moment. Pray prayers of encouragement and thanksgiving for their life. Provide tissues if needed.

For detailed guidelines on responding with prayer, see "Appendix B: A Guide to Praying For Each Other" in this handbook.

WHAT IF WE ARE ALL HAVING A HARD TIME READING SCRIPTURE?

If multiple of you are repeatedly showing up not having read your Bibles, make a shift in your discipleship group. Instead of continuing to answer the Scripture question in the negative, set aside the first 20 minutes of your gatherings to read Scripture together over the next several weeks. Use the alternate Discipleship Group Guide, which outlines how to have a discipleship group in this way. You can find this guide in the "Discipleship Groups" section of this handbook or online at *frontlinechurch.com/discipleship*.

To read Scripture together, select one of the provided reading plans and use the following steps.

1. Briefly pray and ask God to open your eyes to see wonderful things in his Word (Ps 119:18)

2. Read the passage out loud together.

3. Take ten minutes to read back over the passage on your own, and look for three things: a **star**, a **question mark**, and an **arrow**. As you read on your own, try to write down one to three things under each category.

   - *A star:* anything that shines out in the passage and draws attention—it can be something important, or something that strikes you.

   - *A question mark:* anything that is hard to understand—something that you would like to be able to ask the author about.

   - *An arrow:* anything that applies personally to your everyday life.

4. Talk about what you wrote down with your group.

   - Each share a star, and discuss

   - Each share a question mark, and then do your best to work out answers together from the passage. Don't feel pressure to come up with an answer for every question right now. *Don't get bogged down here!*

   - Each share an arrow, and discuss.

WHAT IF SOMEONE DOMINATES THE CONVERSATION? / WHAT IF SOMEONE SAYS SOMETHING UNBIBLICAL? / WHAT IF SOMEONE IS FREQUENTLY ABSENT OR DISENGAGED?

These are common questions that come up in both discipleship groups and family meals. You can find detailed answers to each of these questions under the "Family Meals FAQ" section of this handbook.

FAMILY MEALS

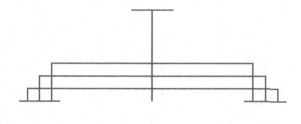

What are the Christian community's meals for? They achieve many things. They express so much of God's grace. They provide a glimpse of what it's like to live under God's reign. They express and reinforce the community that Christ has created through the cross. They're a foretaste of the new creation. They're a great context in which to invite unbelievers so they encounter the reality of God among us. But they're not "for" any of these things. It's a trick question.

Everything else—creation, redemption, mission—is "for" this: that we might eat together in the presence of God. God created the world so we might eat with him. The food we consume, the table around which we sit, and the companions gathered with us have as their end our communion with one another and with God. The Israelites were redeemed to eat with God on the mountain, and we're redeemed for the great messianic banquet that we anticipate when we eat together as a Christian community. We proclaim Christ in mission so that others might hear the invitation to join the feast.

TIM CHESTER
A Meal with Jesus

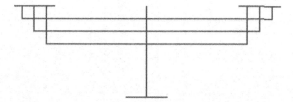

FAMILY MEALS

Casual gatherings around a common table for the sake of community and gospel hospitality

WHAT IS A FAMILY MEAL?

Real-life conversations happen in real-life situations. Some of the best conversations happen around the dinner table or while we're washing the dishes. For our family meals, we set aside an entire evening to prepare, eat, and clean up a meal together. As we linger over the meal, we listen, talk, and pray. Slowly, over time, we can become friends, and—on a deeper level—family. As we eat a meal together, we have the opportunity to experience true community. Participating in a meal together is a symbol of our fellowship and relationship with one another. If we are willing, we can learn one another's stories, vocations, and passions. Quite simply, we become a spiritual family as we practice the "one anothers" of Scripture.

At Frontline, our community groups typically meet for family meal twice a month, on the first and third week of the month. This gathering centers around the meal—preparing, eating, and cleaning up together as a community. A family meal will look different from one community group to the next. We may spend the evening praying for one another. Sometimes, we may talk about what Jesus is teaching us or what we learned from the most recent sermon. And other times, we may just spend time getting to know one another better. However it looks, we pursue the same purpose: to live out our identity as a spiritual family.

One of the great advantages in gathering this way is that it frees people up to be themselves. You don't have to act a certain way or have a certain knowledge set. You don't need to have listened to a sermon or have a curriculum. Anyone can join in— even an outsider who doesn't know Jesus.

At a family meal, we can invite friends, family, co-workers, and non-believers to meet our group and experience God's grace in a less intimidating setting. In pursuit of the Great Commission, we need other avenues for inviting people to experience Christian community besides simply inviting them to a Sunday worship gathering. While some people might be hesitant to set foot inside a church building, they are more likely to show up at a family meal and experience the love of Jesus. Mission is best carried out in the context of community.

> *Simply put, we don't grow or go alone.*

Family meals afford us a unique opportunity to proclaim the gospel and move out on mission where we live. Whenever someone who doesn't follow Jesus pulls up a chair, our family meals shift to offer hospitality and embrace the outsider. In this way, through the warmth of table fellowship, an appetite for spiritual family may be awakened in those far from God. Our hope is that non-Christians might experience the love Christians have for one another—as followers of Jesus serve and care for each other, people can see gospel community in action. When we share the good news of Jesus with them, they will already have a framework for how the gospel impacts lives and relationships.

We push back darkness better when we push it back together. But that means that our community groups can't just consist of Bible studies and prayer meetings. They must also function as kingdom outposts. As we gather around a common table, we provide a glimpse of the coming kingdom of God. And we invite those far from God to join the feast.

HOW DO WE HAVE A FAMILY MEAL?

A family meal will look different from one community group to the next. What one group does, another may do completely differently—yet hopefully they are pursuing the same purpose. For the family meal, we seek to live out our identity as a spiritual family. While there is not a uniform way to accomplish this goal, here are some practical suggestions:

When should we meet for a family meal?
At Frontline, our community groups typically meet for family meal twice a month, on the first and third week of the month. This helps cut down some of the stress of having a weekly large gathering. Find a day of the week that works best for most people in the group, if at all possible. Pick a time that won't put everyone under a time crunch. For groups that have small kids, be aware of how late your group will meet and have an agreed-upon end-time. But, at the end of the day, no day and time will be ideal for everyone. Use your best judgment, and ask your group to commit to regularly engage this rhythm of community.

How do you plan the meal?
For the meal itself, it might work best for one family or person in your community to do the meal planning, but to involve others in the preparation. This cuts down on a lot of the planning and communication that is often necessary to do a potluck-style meal (and also limits the number of leftovers that get left behind). Some community groups may decide to rotate through who is taking point to share the burden over time. As you plan the meal, be aware of any dietary restrictions in your group, or for guests who may be coming. Some easy-to-prepare meals that have worked well for others are homemade individual pizzas, oven-roasted chicken tacos, lasagna and other pasta dishes, or grilling with a variety of salad options. But there are innumerable options that could work equally well.

What does the family meal look like?
Again, each community group will look slightly different. But they will all center around preparing a meal together, eating together, and having gospel-centered conversations. When the meal is ready, you might consider gathering in the kitchen and inviting the host family to pray for the meal. At this point, you may provide some topic of discussion for the dinner. Depending on the dynamics of the group, you may be able to have a more focused conversation, or you may have several smaller informal conversations going on at once. At the end of the evening, consider inviting people to help with clean-up before everyone heads home. Again, the goal of family meal is to gather around a common table for the sake of community, and to live out our identity as a spiritual family. How we accomplish this is flexible and will look different from group to group.

What should we talk about at family meal?
There are a few different options for how to encourage meaningful conversation at a family meal. It is important to ask the question "Who will be there?" We want to be a community where those who aren't yet following Jesus have the opportunity to belong before they believe, and part of that is considering what you talk about.

Discussion could be more informal and focused on what Jesus is teaching us, or on simply getting to know one another better. Often, rather than having a standard Bible study, you can simply ask the question "What was a high and low for you over the past week or two?" This is a great opportunity for those who are believers to speak about God, the gospel, and the Word, and it's also an accessible question for anyone, regardless of their faith, to answer. Other times, we may have a discussion about the most recent sermon. If you do, consider doing it in such a way that anyone can meaningfully participate in the conversation. Summarize what the sermon was about and ask an open-ended question.

Finally, you may dedicate your whole gathering to checking in and praying for one another. Praying together can be a catalyst for deeper community and love for one another. Regardless of the topic, you shouldn't feel pressure to lead the discussion every time. If someone in your group is great at leading discussion, let them do so occasionally. You could still help direct the content and focus of the conversation.

FAMILY MEAL PRAYER NIGHT

Family meals can occasionally be dedicated to praying together as a community group. While a prayer gathering can go a number of different directions, one option is to hold a kingdom-focused prayer night geared towards the city. When having a prayer night as a community group, there are a few guidelines for etiquette that are important to communicate to everyone beforehand:

- **Make room for different prayer postures.** Whether a person sits, stands, kneels, or raises hands, everyone should seek to engage their hearts as well as their bodies.

- **Prayer doesn't have to go around in a circle.** Instead, pray spontaneously as you feel willing. Sometimes, a person may pray multiple times before someone else prays.

- **As you pray, listen for what the Holy Spirit may be speaking.** The Holy Spirit often gives words, pictures, and Scriptures to help guide the prayer time. If you sense something, share it and let it guide your prayers.

- **Don't rush to fill the silence.** There will be times when everyone engages silently, and that's okay. In these moments, God is often profoundly working.

- **Pray in everyday language.** You don't have to polish your prayers or change the tone of your voice when praying.

- **Ground your prayers in Scripture.** Don't just let those words inspire you, but fill your prayers with the words of Scripture.

- **Have an assigned facilitator.** Typically this will be a community group leader or apprentice who leads through the movements and closes out the time.

- **Avoid "rock pile" prayers.** These are prayers where everyone merely tosses disconnected prayers on the pile. Instead work to maintain a unified focus in your prayer together. Introducing a new theme

of prayer every ten to fifteen minutes will help in this regard. As thematic focus begins to drift, it is usually a sign that a particular prayer theme has been sufficiently explored, and it is time for the facilitator to introduce the next theme.

The following outlines an example of a kingdom-focused prayer night, taking roughly ten to fifteen minutes for each movement. For each movement, read the Scripture out loud, then use the prayer points for guidance. When it is time to move on, the facilitator will lead into the next movement.

1. Praying for the Community Group

And day by day, attending the temple together and breaking bread in their homes, they received their food with glad and generous hearts, praising God and having favor with all the people. And the Lord added to their number day by day those who were being saved. - Acts 2:46-47

Prayer Points:

- Pray for the people in your life who don't follow Jesus, such as your "three."
- Pray for the neighborhood around where you live.
- Pray that the group would love and serve the community well.

2. Praying for the Church

To me, though I am the very least of all the saints, this grace was given, to preach to the Gentiles the unsearchable riches of Christ, and to bring to light for everyone what is the plan of the mystery hidden for ages in God, who created all things, so that through the church the manifold wisdom of God might now be made known to the rulers and authorities in the heavenly places. - Ephesians 3:8-10

Prayer Points:

- Pray for the church to have a gospel impact in the city.

- Pray for the church to be marked by missional faithfulness.
- Pray for the church to be a light of the gospel in the midst of darkness.

3. Praying for the City

But seek the welfare of the city where I have sent you into exile, and pray to the LORD on its behalf, for in its welfare you will find your welfare.
- Jeremiah 29:7

Prayer Points:

- Pray for workplaces, schools, non-profits, and other places in our city, that they would experience the blessing of God.
- Pray for our local, state, and national government officials.
- Pray for revival and renewal to impact our city.

FAMILY MEALS FAQ

HOW DO WE CARE FOR CHILDREN DURING A FAMILY MEAL?

It is important that the community group makes a joint decision on how to care for children during a family meal. Community groups can connect children to healthy relationships with adults outside their family and provide opportunities to model discipleship for parents who feel ill-equipped to disciple their own children.

Because a family meal allows us to live out our identity as a spiritual family, we should integrate our children into this time, wherever it makes sense. Families are rarely neat and tidy, and children are a part of normal family dynamics. Also, some of our children may be followers of Jesus and called to experience spiritual family as well. But the degree of child involvement will vary depending on age and maturity. One option is to keep them involved in everything you do—from prayer, to eating, to sharing stories—all the way to cleaning up. Another option is to feed the kids separately and allow them to play together, while the adults share a meal of their own and spend time with one another.

There may be times when paying for childcare is optimal for your group. If and when that is the case, please consider the following:

- When planning for child care, use wisdom and discretion. Child care workers, whether paid or volunteer, should be well-vetted. This includes, but is not limited to, obtaining references, performing background checks, setting up clear accountability, and ensuring that the workers are competent.

- Have the group collectively provide finances for vetted childcare. Be sure to pay attention to caregiver/child ratios. Don't overwhelm your caregiver with too many children. If necessary, employ more than one worker.

- For accountability and safety reasons, it is wise to have two adults from two different households to care for the children while the group meets. Members of your group may rotate on a schedule. Do not allow a child care worker to be alone with a child who is not their own. This is for the worker's safety as much as the child's.

- As an option, you could host child care at one location and gather at another. If the two are geographically close, allow trusted caregivers to provide care at one location while the group meets at the other.

WHAT IF SOMEONE DOMINATES THE CONVERSATION?

Community groups often have one or two people who tend to dominate the conversation with their assertive personalities. And while what they say can often be good or helpful, they don't always create an environment where others feel the freedom, or have the space, to join the conversation. When that is the case, here are some steps you can take to have a more fruitful discussion:

Use your best judgment to assess the situation. There are moments where it is appropriate and good for someone to share at length about what they are experiencing. Maybe something is weighing heavy on them, or they are going through a tough season. Always ask yourself: "Is it appropriate to set aside extended time to care for this person, or do we need to hear from others?"

Redirect the conversation to encourage others to share. This may look like calling on a specific person to chime in with their thoughts. Or taking a moment to reopen the conversation to everyone. For example, you may say, "John, those are some really great thoughts. I'd love to hear what some others would have to say. Stacy, we haven't heard from you. What are you thinking?"

Take a moment at the beginning of the discussion to encourage those who are hesitant to share. Some people have a deep fear of sharing their thoughts with a group of people. Others are internal processors and simply need a moment to think about the question. For both groups of people, it is important to communicate that you value what they bring to the conversation. Sometimes, it can be helpful to ask hesitant people if they have anything they would like to share, while also giving them space to say "no." Recognize that when these people share in a group, it is often an act of courage that should be welcomed and celebrated. It is also important to let people know that silence is okay. Sometimes it takes a minute for people to think, and we don't have to fill the silence.

If someone continues to dominate the conversation, have a private conversation with that person. Some people are just not aware that they are dominating the conversation, or how the family meal conversation should flow. First, seek to encourage and bless this person. Thank them for their contributions to the group, recognizing their insights with specificity. Confirm their desire to speak as valuable. Second, point out to them that we want to create an environment where everyone has the opportunity to share in the family meal conversation. Encourage them to continue sharing, but ask them to give space to allow others to speak and contribute. Be sure to give this person an opportunity to respond to what you've said and pray with them. Be prepared to have this conversation more than once. Don't take offense or assume high-handed sin if you have to revisit and remind more than once.

WHAT IF SOMEONE SAYS SOMETHING UNBIBLICAL?

From time to time, you will likely have a group member give a response to a discussion question that is either biblically inaccurate, or even heretical. How should you respond in such instances? Here are some practical steps to consider:

Discern the nature of what is being said. There is a world of difference between being incorrect and being heretical or unbiblical. For instance, someone may simply misunderstand or misapply a passage in a way it wasn't intended. If what they say is confirmed in other parts of Scripture, there is no need to heavy-handedly correct them. On the other hand, someone may espouse something that is directly contrary to the Bible's primary teachings on the person and work of Jesus or our salvation. Such cases require gentle correction.

If they made a minor mistake, avoid immediate correction. Your group should be a safe place to share, and a quick reaction could discourage full participation and willingness among members. In many cases, if what they said was biblical but slightly misapplied, you can let it go. If it feels important for you to address the error, pull them aside privately after the discussion. You can say something along the lines of, "Thank you for engaging the discussion! What you said was good and insightful. But I also think there is another way to look at this passage. I think the context of that particular verse means..."

If they say something that directly contradicts Scripture, gently correct them in the midst of the discussion. It is important to remember that most people are not saying things maliciously. Many times, they have been taught incorrectly, or they have never thought through the implications of that false belief. Depending on the situation, you may just ask the rest of the group their thoughts on the topic. Usually, someone will provide correction in a natural way. The person who originally made the statement will see that they were out of line with biblical truth without feeling singled out. In other situations, you could correct the statement, while also affirming their willingness to participate. You can say something as simple as, "Thank you for your thoughts! I see where you are coming from, but I don't think that is quite right because of _____. I think a better way to understand this text would be _____."

If you need to correct someone, follow up with them after the discussion. Pull them aside to once again affirm their willingness to participate and share what they are thinking. Extend an invitation for you both to discuss the topic more thoroughly together. Reaffirm your love and care for them.

WHAT IF SOMEONE IS FREQUENTLY ABSENT OR DISENGAGED?

Taking the time to reach out to someone shows them that they are valued and not just a face in the crowd. Since community is an essential part of a healthy Christian life, we should encourage one another to maintain relationship whenever any of us begin to drift away. Missing one family meal is not usually a big deal. But if someone has missed three family meals with no word, that would definitely constitute a need to reach out. An off-color comment might pique your interest and require a follow-up question. A revelation of need might require action. The occasions for follow-up vary, but they require attentive eyes and ears to notice and act on them.

You can follow up with them through a text, a phone call, or an in-person conversation. The method of communication will depend significantly on the situation. Did someone just miss a single gathering? You could shoot them a text to let them know the group missed them. Has it been a few weeks since you've seen them? It might be good to give them a phone call. Does it feel like someone is in the process of leaving the church? That probably requires a face-to-face interaction. Use your best judgment, and feel free to rely on your hub leader for direction.

Sometimes, a person's lack of attendance settles into a long-term pattern of inconsistency. While this can become frustrating, it is important to have a caring conversation, rather than assume they are apathetic or disgruntled. Our hearts are quicker to assign motives than to seek truth. When you notice this pattern of inconsistency, set aside time to have a conversation and ask them about their absence. Allow them space to share what they are experiencing, and offer to help where appropriate. Let them know that you value them both as a person and as a part of the group.

When having this kind of follow-up conversation with someone who is habitually absent or disengaged, here are a few things to keep in mind:

- *Be prompt.* Don't wait too long to reach out once you notice the pattern. If you forget to reach out and time passes, push through the awkwardness. It will mean that much more that you cared enough to make it happen.

- *Make space to listen.* "Seek first to understand before seeking to be understood." Don't make accusations based on assumptions. Rather, listen to them and give room for them to be heard if there is an issue. Ask questions like "I've noticed you've been missing family meal a lot. What is going on in your life?" and "How can I be praying for you and encouraging you during this time?"

- *Maintain a loving tone.* How you say something can often outlast the actual words you say. This is not a conversation to pass judgment, but to actively seek how best to care for them in this season of their life. It should elicit compassion and patient love. Don't forget, they are souls to be cared for.

- *Stress the importance of community.* After listening for an extended period of time, where appropriate, encourage the individual with truths from God's Word about the importance of community and commitment (Matt. 22:37-40; Heb. 3:12-13; 10:23-25).

- *Know when to stop.* Do your part to communicate what they need to hear. There is no need to coerce them or badger them into engaging more. If they seem unreceptive after you have communicated your concerns, let the conversation breathe and give them time to process and consider what has been shared.

- *Be patient.* Give them time to adjust after the conversation. Trust the Lord to move and work. Encourage them where it seems they are taking more initiative and showing up more.

- *Fill in your hub leader.* It is important to let your hub leader know about care issues going on in your group. If you have concerns about someone's attendance, or if you need to have one of these follow-up conversations, contact your hub leader and allow them to speak into the situation.

MISSIONAL GATHERINGS

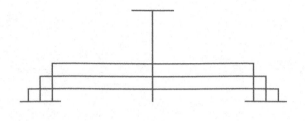

If the gospel is to challenge the public life of our society, if Christians are to occupy the "high ground" which they vacated in the noon time of "modernity," it will not be by forming a Christian political party, or by aggressive propaganda campaigns... It will only be by movements that begin with the local congregation in which the reality of the new creation is present, known, and experienced, and from which men and women will go into every sector of public life to claim it for Christ, to unmask the illusions which have remained hidden and to expose all areas of public life to the illumination of the gospel. But that will only happen as and when local congregations renounce an introverted concern for their own life, and recognize that they exist for the sake of those who are not members, as sign, instrument, and foretaste of God's redeeming grace for the whole life of society.

LESSLIE NEWBIGIN
The Gospel in a Pluralist Society

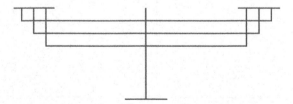

MISSIONAL GATHERINGS

*Gathering intentionally for the sake of people far from God
to proclaim the gospel and demonstrate the kingdom*

WHAT IS A MISSIONAL GATHERING?

In addition to our own growth and development, community groups exist so that others might come to know and follow Jesus. Missional gatherings help us push back darkness through both gospel proclamation and kingdom demonstration. Missional gatherings give us the opportunity to build relationships with those who don't follow Jesus and tell them about the one who has rescued us. They also give us the opportunity to care for the spiritual and physical needs of those in darkness around us.

Recalling his time living among and ministering to the believers in Thessalonica, Paul writes in 1 Thessalonians 2:8, "...being affectionately desirous of you, we were ready to share with you not only the gospel of God but also our own selves, because you had become very dear to us." According to this passage, we see a beautifully balanced "both-and" of pushing back darkness through gospel proclamation and kingdom demonstration. It corrects the tendency to only share the gospel abruptly with strangers—answering questions they may not even be asking. But it also corrects the tendency to view evangelism as arrogant and self-righteous.

None of us naturally drift into mission. It takes great intentionality to make time for people outside our community. Obedience means gathering for the sake of people who don't know Jesus. Mission is ultimately about people, not projects. We must think through ways we can integrate people into our communities, and not just serve them at arm's length. At Frontline, we repeatedly proclaim (and rightly so) that we are A Church For the City. The more we serve our city, participate in the life of our city, and proclaim the gospel to our city, the more we will fulfill the promise embedded in that statement.

To engage our city on mission, we must introduce people into the daily life of the church—into Christian community. The gospel message must be adorned with the conduct of gospel community. As onlookers see the power of the gospel with their own eyes, it will often provoke curiosity. Many of us view mission in isolation from community—such that we end up living on mission individually, with little crossover. This puts unbelievable pressure on each one of us to be an expert in mission. Instead, those who don't follow Jesus should be invited to hang out with Christians who are hanging out with other Christians. This has always been Jesus' vision for melting hearts. "By this all people will know that you are my disciples, if you have love for one another" (Jn 13:35). The interpersonal love of the Christian community is, in the words of Francis Schaeffer, "the ultimate apologetic." Missional gatherings make these kinds of encounters possible.

WHY DO WE ENGAGE IN MISSION?

In the Church, it is popular to talk about living on mission and being a "missional" church. But often, we don't explain what we mean by mission, which leads to general confusion. For some Christians, "mission" is synonymous with evangelism. For others, "mission" has more to do with serving the needy in our communities. Still others see "mission" as the Church's work internationally, to bring the gospel to unreached places. While all of these capture an aspect of the Church's mission, none of them fully encapsulate what the Bible teaches about mission.

Mission isn't first and foremost grounded in Matthew 28, as important as the Great Commission is. Mission is grounded in Genesis 1, and it permeates the whole

Bible. The mission of the Church finds its roots in the very mission that God has been actively working towards through all of history. In the beginning, God created the universe with a mission: to fill all creation with his blessing and presence. To this end, all of creation was designed to reflect the heart of God— his goodness and character and attributes.

As the pinnacle of his creation, God uniquely created man and woman in his image. They were royal representatives of God on earth, charged with a special mission: to rule over creation and fill it with God's blessing. Yet even as his original intention for creation seemed to be unraveling because of our sin, God set to work to fulfill his mission through redemption and restoration. He would redeem humanity from their sin, and he would restore his blessing to his creation. And he was going to accomplish this mission through his people. In short, we engage in mission because we were created for it.

If we only discuss strategies and techniques for reaching people far from God, and skip right over the motivation required to sustain that mission, we will never overcome the inconvenience and sacrifice required to gather for the sake of people far from God. Identity precedes action. If we don't have a settled sense in our hearts that we are adopted sons and daughters of the Father, we will never be able to keep our hand to the gospel plow. We have been called into a spiritual family, and we have been called out on God's mission. Paul says "we are ambassadors for Christ, God making his appeal through us" (2 Cor 5:20). We have been called and commissioned to "implore" our friends and neighbors "on behalf of Christ, be reconciled to God" because of the great good news that "for our sake he made him to be sin who knew no sin, so that in him we might become the righteousness of God" (1 Cor 5:20–21)!

WHAT DO MISSIONAL GATHERINGS LOOK LIKE?

First, we gather missionally to *host*. We gather with the expressed intention of showing gospel hospitality to those outside of Christian community. Hospitality builds trust and encourages conversations to go deeper. Acquaintances might even become friends. Hosting could be as simple as throwing a block party or engaging some cultural event, such as Halloween or the Super Bowl. Or it could look like inviting one of your neighbors to your next family meal. Whatever it looks like, we hope that through hosting, our presence would begin to be felt in our neighborhood.

Second, we gather missionally to *help*. We prioritize serving with our City Partners, which are organizations thoughtfully chosen by each congregation on the basis of their impact. As we serve the poor, marginalized, and needy in our communities, we build relationships with our community. Since many non-Christians also have a desire to do good for their city, we can invite them to serve alongside us as a means of strengthening our friendship. Each congregation can help equip our community groups to engage their unique City Partners.

There are needs all around us, even right next door. We have the opportunity to show the love of Jesus to our neighbors and friends by serving them and caring for them. Maybe we have a neighborhood cookout to further engage those in our community. Or we get permission to help a neighbor rebuild their fence. Or we figure out ways to serve a local school in our area. As we thoughtfully engage where we live, we will notice people and places where we can bring the light of Jesus to the world. We provide Push Back Darkness Grants to our community groups to empower them to meet specific needs in their own community.

Finally, we gather missionally to *hang out*. We gather regularly with those who don't follow Jesus in natural, neutral places outside of the church and our homes. This helps us form new friendships and introduce people to Christian community, while we gather with people where they already go. This could be at a coffee shop, a park, a concert, or some other event. It could be centered around a hobby or another recreational activity. Regardless, the point is to look for less-intimidating places where we can build relationships with non-Christians. These gatherings organically fit into the rhythms of others' lives. We should invite our unbelieving friends, family, and neighbors to gather with us as we have fun together and get to know one another. It should feel informal and non-committal for those we invite. The hope is that through these missional gatherings, over time, we will have organic opportunities to speak about Jesus.

Missional gatherings are a great opportunity to include children. Not only will they be discipled as they serve alongside others in the group, but it will also help them see that they are never too young to contribute to God's mission. Use wisdom and make sure they are engaging in ways that are appropriate for their age and maturity-level.

MISSIONAL GATHERINGS FAQ

HOW DO WE PLAN A MISSIONAL GATHERING?

Often, community groups want to start gathering missionally, but they don't know how to get started. Here are a few ideas.

- *Start slowly and be realistic.* Community groups don't become missional overnight. Talk as a group, and pick one place to start. Maybe it is a gathering in a neutral place. Maybe it is a service project with a City Partner. Often it is better to plan a smaller gathering rather than something that everyone does together. Whatever it is, pick one thing and agree to prayerfully and patiently begin walking it out together. It is okay if things don't go as planned, or if only a few people can make it.

- *Find out what everyone is already involved in.* Chances are that people in your group are already gathering somewhere in your city. Some may even be regularly involved in serving with a non-profit. Instead of adding something new, find out what people are already doing, and invite the rest of the group to join them.

- *Ask questions of geography and affinity.* While mission always requires sacrifice, from another perspective, gathering missionally in your community requires asking two simple questions: "Where do the people we want to reach already spend time and naturally go?" and "How can we gather there as a group?" Think through your own passions and interests, where you love to go and what you love to do in your area of the city. Are there specific issues you care about or communities you have a desire to serve? Talk about these together and explore ideas where there is mutual interest and crossover.

- *Leave with action steps.* Sometimes, community groups can get stuck trying to plan a missional gathering. One way to get things moving is to leave the discussion with action steps, deadlines, and point people. Action steps could include sending out communication, contacting a City Partner, applying for a Push Back Darkness Grant, or scheduling a date. Before wrapping up the discussion, talk about what action steps need to be taken, who will do them, and when they should be done.

- *Invite your "three" and other non-Christians to each missional gathering.* Your group should not gather missionally to the exclusion of others. Instead, we want to show hospitality and deepen our relationship with those far from Jesus. If the missional gathering is in a neutral place, invite your "three" to gather with you. Prepare to be welcoming and conversational with any unbelievers that attend. If the missional gathering is a service opportunity, invite them to serve alongside you, where appropriate.

HOW DO WE GET CONNECTED TO OUR CITY PARTNERS?

Each congregation has their own unique City Partners. These are organizations doing great work throughout our city, thoughtfully chosen by each congregation as a place for missional impact. Reach out to your hub leader or community director to find out your congregation's specific City Partners and how your group can get connected to serve.

WHAT ARE PUSH BACK DARKNESS GRANTS?

Push Back Darkness Grants provide financial assistance to our community groups so they can meet needs and show the love of Jesus to their community. Our hope is that as you and others in your group see specific needs in your neighborhood with your own eyes, you would prayerfully discern how you might meet those needs, and take concrete steps to push back darkness. With Push Back Darkness Grants, groups have repainted the homes of single moms, built wheelchair ramps for the disabled, and renovated teacher lounges for schools in need. Any community group has the opportunity to apply for a grant. To apply for a Push Back Darkness Grant:

Fill out the online application. Visit *frontlinechurch.com/grants* and select your congregation. Fill out the application and be prepared to answer the following questions:

- What is the project? How does it focus on serving the poor in our city? How might it initiate or strengthen relational ministry to a family or community? Will a City Partner be involved?

- What is the total cost of the project? How much assistance are you requesting? How is your community group planning to contribute to meeting this need?

- Specify a breakdown of how the grant will be spent if awarded.

Wait for next steps. After you submit the application, someone on staff will contact you with next steps. Be patient! Depending on the details of the grant request, your pastors will probably need to discuss and decide on an action step or two. However, if you haven't heard anything after a week, feel free to reach out to a hub leader and ask for an update.

WHO ARE MY "THREE"?

For many people, the thought of engaging unbelievers can feel overwhelming. We may think, "Do I know enough to convince someone about the good news of Jesus? There are so many people who don't follow Jesus in the world. Where do I even begin?" These thoughts can be paralyzing. But it is important to remember a few things. First, we are limited beings, bound by time and space. We can't be everywhere for everyone. Second, God often uses relationships with Christians to draw an unbeliever's heart to him. Third, we can take small steps to more faithfully engage in mission.

To this end, we recommend our members focus on their "three." These are three people within their sphere of influence who do not follow Jesus or are not connected to a local church. We ask everyone to commit to pray daily for their "three" and engage them in intentional gospel relationships. These people could be children, family, friends, co-workers,

neighbors, or others. As a starting point, work through the following exercise with your group:

1. Identify your "three." Take five minutes to prayerfully and thoughtfully select and write down the names of three people in your life who do not follow Jesus or are not connected to a local church. Whom would you most love to see become a disciple of Jesus? Who is your heart best shaped to reach for Jesus?

If you are having difficulty identifying three people, it could be an invitation to more thoughtfully engage friendships with those who don't follow Jesus. Spending meaningful time in places other than your workplace, home, and church can help you form new friendships. Or perhaps you might need to approach places you frequent with greater gospel intentionality. Maybe you regularly interact with non-Christians at coffee shops and sporting events. A hobby might bring you shoulder-to-shoulder with those far from God. How might you intentionally move towards those people and deepen your friendship with them?

Once you've identified three people (or as many people as you can), for each person in turn, answer the following questions posed by missiologist Alan Hirsch:

- Am I in close proximity with this person to whom I feel called?

- Am I spending regular time with this person? If not, why not?

- Am I too busy to develop a meaningful relationship with this person? If so, how could I create margin for mission?

2. Share with your community group. Go around and briefly share at least one of the people you selected, and why you chose them. If any of you are struggling to identify someone in your life, invite the group to process with you who you might identify.

3. Pray for your "three." Conclude your time by praying out loud for the people you have named—especially for your relationships to grow and deepen with them, for God to give you all creativity in how to spend regular time with them, and for God to give your community group opportunities to collectively love them, serve them, and share the gospel with them.

4. Revisit your "three." Write down the names of your "three" with a marker on some physical object that will not be easily lost, and that can be pulled back out for future gatherings. Be creative! A leftover piece of floor tile, a thrift store painting, or a commemorative plate, can serve as a humorous and memorable way to capture and keep your focus on praying for and pursuing your "three."

WHAT ARE COMMON BARRIERS TO LIVING ON MISSION?

I don't have any non-Christian friends. If we are not careful, we can end up spending all our time in "Christian" circles. As a result, it can be difficult for followers of Jesus to form meaningful relationships with people far from God. But in order to be a church for the city, we have to get to know the people around us, and learn how to be good friends to our neighbors. Where do you currently interact with those far from God? Where do you live, work, and play? How can you make a step towards deepening your relationship with those already around you?

We tend to *underestimate* how lonely most people are, and we tend to *overestimate* how much they will resist our overtures of friendship. If we thought more in terms of making friends with people far from God, and we thought less transactionally about evangelism, we would realize that we know far more about being ambassadors for Christ than our fears and insecurities would lead us to believe.

If you can be a friend, you can be on mission.

Non-Christians don't come to the things I invite them to. In an increasingly post-Christian West, "Come and see" is not enough—we must also "Go and tell." It takes a lot of courage for non-Christians to step out of their comfort zone and attend a "church" function. Yet for many of us, this tends to be our primary method of evangelism. And while some people will be open to these invitations, most will be hesitant until they first know and trust us. We shouldn't require them to do something we aren't willing to do ourselves. We often require people to come to us, attend our events, and initiate relationship. Instead, we should be the ones going out to them. We should be willing to step out of our

comfort zone as we invite them to do the same. We deepen our relationships with non-Christians as we serve in our city and participate in what is already happening. Service and participation are humble acts that increasingly lead us out of our comfort and out of ourselves.

I'm scared to share the gospel. Sharing the gospel can be intimidating. We worry we won't have all the answers. We worry we won't say the right thing. But it is important to remember that God is the one who saves people, not us, and not merely our words. Many of us came to faith when someone imperfectly shared the gospel with us. We don't have to have all the answers. We can share our hope in Jesus, and trust him to work in this person's heart.

We also must remember the importance of community for mission. The experience of Christian community is often a catalyst for reception of the gospel. Hearing about the gospel is one thing. Seeing it in the lives of Christians, who are being transformed by the love of Christ, is another.

I don't have time for mission. Mission always begins with making room for God to come in. If we are operating with little to no margin in our lives, we might hear the call to live on mission as added homework. However, living on mission is often less about doing more, and more about doing it differently, with different people, or in a different place.

How might God be calling you to simplify your life in order to create margin? Before we can be boldly strategic in our pursuit of the lost, we will first need to fight to live simpler lives. God is already on mission where we live, work, and play. But we are often in too much of a hurry, and too focused on ourselves, to notice his repeated invitation to join him in pursuing people with whom we interact every day, every week, every month.

A LIFE ON MISSION
(FOR ORDINARY PEOPLE)

A LIFE ON MISSION
(FOR ORDINARY PEOPLE)

HOW SHOULD WE THINK ABOUT JESUS' INVITATION TO JOIN HIM ON HIS MISSION?

We ought to view ourselves as "ambassadors for Christ" (2 Cor 5:20). But consider some of the emotions we typically feel when we hear someone talk about the mission of God, or evangelism, or missional living, or naming and pursuing our "three." Contrary to what you might feel in the pit of your stomach whenever this topic is raised, the good news is that:

- Growing as ambassadors is less about adding homework and more about adding *margin*.

- Growing as ambassadors is less about doing our duty and more about our duty being transformed into *delight*.

- Growing as ambassadors is less about gritting our teeth and more about growing in *gratitude*.

Jesus' invitation is not to white-knuckle or manufacture mission. God's not asking us to leap tall missional buildings in a single bound, or transform ourselves into something we're not. So how should we think about Jesus' invitation to join him on his mission? If not as added homework, then what?

The standing invitation running through the whole New Testament is to act who we are with the Spirit's help—to bring who we are and how we live into greater congruence, so that who we are in Christ, and how we live in light of that identity, match up more and more over time.

C. S. Lewis brilliantly points out that when we don't understand the difference between doing our duty out of guilt, versus being given new desires by God, then we tend to respond to Jesus like weary tax-payers. We pay up because we don't want to be audited or punished, but the whole time, Lewis says, we're secretly hoping we'll have enough left over to live on. But if we keep doing that, one of two things will happen—either we'll give up trying to obey, or we'll become miserable. Notice what he says:

The Christian way is different: harder, and easier. Christ says 'Give me All. I don't want so much of your time and so much of your money and so much of your work: I want You. I have not come to torment your natural self, but to kill it. No half-measures are any good. I don't want to cut off a branch here and a branch there, I want to have the whole tree down... Hand over the whole natural self, all the desires which you think innocent as well as the ones you think wicked—the whole outfit. I will give you a new self instead. In fact, I will give you Myself: my own will shall become yours.'

Both harder and easier than what we are all trying to do. You have noticed, I expect, that Christ Himself sometimes describes the Christian way as very hard, sometimes as very easy. He says, 'Take up your Cross'—in other words, it is like going to be beaten to death in a concentration camp. Next minute he says, 'My yoke is easy and my burden light.' He means both. And one can just see why both are true. (C. S. Lewis, *Mere Christianity*)

We won't make room for the mission of God in a real or lasting way if we're driven by guilt or duty. We'll only make room for the mission of God if we're motivated by our deepest desires. And that's why the answer to the question of how we should think about Jesus' invitation to join him on his mission is that it's more about added heart work than added homework.

HOW DO WE START WHERE WE ACTUALLY ARE, INSTEAD OF WHERE WE THINK WE OUGHT TO BE?

When it comes to the mission of God, not only do we tend to think that we just need to do more and try harder, but we also tend to confuse our real self with our *ideal* self.

One of the most common ways people injure themselves when they start a new workout regimen is by trying to lift too much, too hard, too fast. Their form quickly unravels after a couple of reps, and then they injure themselves. If they'd just been honest, and humbled themselves, and started with the proper amount of weight—regardless if the pregnant woman next to them was effortlessly throwing up three times as much weight—they could have avoided injuring themselves, getting discouraged, and dropping out.

Much of the discouragement and failure we experience as ambassadors comes from starting where we think we *ought* to be instead of starting where we actually are. Instead of trying to radically reinvent yourself overnight, you can start by doing two simple things: (1) regularly participate in a discipleship group, and (2) pray for your "three" when you're together. We've never seen someone who begins to pray for their "three," alongside other Christians, who doesn't begin to see God move—first in *their* hearts, and *then* in the hearts of their "three."

A friend of ours was once looking out the back window of his house at all his neighbors' fences, reflecting on how difficult it has become to meet your neighbors and build friendships in modern suburbia. He suddenly found himself praying "Lord, tear down all the fences." God answered his prayer both metaphorically and literally. Within a year, his neighbors began to hit it off with him and each other to such a degree that they all spontaneously agreed to take down the sections of their fences facing each other so their kids could play together more easily, and they could all cook out and hang out together more easily, and God began to open doors for kingdom demonstration and gospel proclamation. And it all started with a one-sentence prayer spoken out of weakness.

All throughout his letters, Paul repeatedly describes his longing to be reunited with those for whom he regularly prays. Your feet will follow your heart. You can't carry someone in your heart and never call them or want to see them. Prayer will slowly turn a neglected duty into a source of delight. *You'll move toward whoever you make the focus of your prayers.*

Start by simply naming and praying for three people far from God that you have the opportunity to see regularly and move towards. People you'd particularly love to see come to faith. People who seem open and responsive to your overtures of friendship.

To better inform our prayers together in our discipleship groups, Alan Hirsch suggests that we continually ask each other three questions:

- Am I in close proximity with these people to whom I feel called?
- Am I spending regular time with them? If not, why not?
- Am I too busy to develop meaningful relationships with them?

HOW DO WE MOVE TOWARDS PEOPLE?

We live in volatile times. Christians are increasingly viewed with suspicion. As we seek to develop meaningful relationships with people far from God, we should assume we'll be starting at a deficit with many of them, but that shouldn't paralyze or discourage us. When we encounter suspicion, we should respond with kindness, and then calmly and quietly set to work building bridges of trust that can bear the weight of truth.

Here are a few principles for moving towards people:

- *Start with facts of public record.* "Where did you grow up?" "What brought you to Oklahoma?" "Any plans this weekend?" "How was work this past week?"

- *Accept all invitations to move the conversation one step deeper.* "I'm originally from Florida, but my parents went through a messy divorce when I was twelve, and my mom moved us here." Why did they tell you that? They didn't have to. "I'm so sorry. That must have been hard."

- *Remember and build on what you know.* If it helps you, write down what you learn and review it before you see them again. Failure to capture names before you forget them is one of the biggest barriers to mission.

- *Vigilantly scan for and vocally affirm any good that you see or hear.* "I've noticed you do a great job supporting your son during the soccer season—you're a good example to the rest of us dads on the street."

- *Be curious, but reserve judgment, and be slow to give advice.* When in doubt, ask one more question.

- *Follow up.* "How did that test turn out?" "How was your presentation?" "How was it going back home for the holiday?

- *Be on the lookout for needs both small and great.* Maybe they need someone to drive them to the hospital for a surgery they're feeling nervous about, so you offer to take them in early in the morning, and if appropriate, you offer to pray for them when you drop them off.

- *Be quick to celebrate, support, and show up.* Do they have an upcoming graduation you can attend? Do they have a birthday coming up? Do you have a birthday coming up? Be quick to accept and extend invitations. Include people far from God in your holidays, hangouts, and celebrations.

- *Affirmation doesn't always have to equal agreement.* Seek to build relational trust before seeking to turn the conversation towards gospel truth. You're not being a coward if you wait to bring correction or speak more candidly about your beliefs, until you've gotten to know each other better.

HOW CAN WE AVOID DEFEAT BEFORE WE EVEN GET STARTED?

We'll need to be aware of, and resist, at least four common barriers that tend to derail well-intended ambassadors early and often.

1. *The barrier of being independent.* We know we can't grow alone, but we forget we can't go alone. Left to ourselves, we each don't have enough spiritual gifts for the people God has called us to pursue.

2. *The barrier of being impersonal.* We can approach our "three" more as projects and less as people. We can be thinking of what we should say next instead of listening deeply. Too often we fall into an unconscious posture of critique, assuming we have to prove to them how their lives are not working without Jesus, so we can win a hearing for the gospel.

3. *The barrier of being impatient.* In order to think biblically, we need to think "agriculture," not "assembly line." We are called to befriend our "three" patiently—regardless of the timeline and expected outcomes in our head. Pursuing people far from God is slow, quiet, uncertain work. It is opaque, and sometimes filled with setbacks and ingratitude, but our love needs to hold steady—even when they don't make the kind of spiritual progress we want to see, when we want to see it.

4. *The barrier of being in control.* The fascinating (and sometimes maddening!) thing about people is that while you can listen to them, serve them, pray for them, be generous to them, forgive them, check on them, and feed them... you can't control them or predict them—or make them more efficient, grateful, or logical. You can't insulate yourself from being affected by them, you can't fast-track them, and you can't whip them into shape. We can accomplish tasks; but we can't accomplish relationships—we can only cultivate them.

HOW DO WE FINISH WELL?

If we're called to be *this* personal and *this* patient, and put up with *this* many surprises and setbacks, we're going to need a kind of inner calm and a kind of inner confidence that can feel a bit unrealistic. How are we supposed to completely rearrange our lives, push past suspicion, avoid all these obstacles, and—on top of all that—somehow not lose heart and drop out along the way?

Walking alongside other people will wake up some fears you didn't even know you had, and some others you've managed to keep down for a long time. How do we make this into a new and permanent way of life instead of merely a forgotten New Year's Resolution? How do we run a marathon instead of a sprint?

One of the most important answers to that question is: *naming our fears out loud to God and other people.* Depending on our story, some will play in the background for us, and others will dominate our thoughts and feelings. Consider which of these might push to the front for you.

- The fear of failure.

- The fear of not knowing whether you're doing a good job.
- The fear of not being enough.
- The fear of not having enough left over to live on.
- The fear of rejection.
- The fear of exposure, embarrassment (shame), and feeling or appearing foolish.
- The fear of losing control.
- The fear of being taken advantage of, manipulated, used, hustled, or fooled.
- The fear of loss of status or judgment in the eyes of others.
- The fear of harm.
- The fear of wasting your time, and having nothing to show for your work.
- The fear of feeling invisible, isolated, alone, and overwhelmed.

When we encounter the chaos and brokenness of someone else's story and we don't like how it feels, we're tempted to lean back. "Never again," we think to ourselves. There's a uniquely American obsession with not being taken advantage of—with not being fooled or being made to feel foolish.

In our experience, most of the time, even something as small and seemingly insignificant as a phone call with a friend who's feeling overwhelmed on mission can work wonders: "You're not alone." "You're doing a great job—don't give up." "I'll come with you." "Let's pray right now." "Let me know how it goes." "Keep me updated." "Who can we add to the team?" "Here's why you're doing a better job than you think you are." "Thank you for what you're doing."

Our fears may have been lying dormant, but moving towards our "three" will inevitably wake them up. As they start rattling the bars of their cage, we have the opportunity to be guided by the Psalms and name our fears out loud to God and to our friends.

CONCLUSION

It's easy to forget that the men and women Jesus gathered around himself in the Gospels and sent out on mission were just as anxious, afraid, reluctant, distracted, confused, overwhelmed, exhausted, and inadequate as you and me. But Paul reminds us that "what we are is known to God" (2 Cor 5:11). When Paul says that "the love of Christ controls us" (2 Cor 5:14)

he means that God's love is so surprising, undeserved, and steady that it melts our hearts, and fills us with grateful, restful joy. In the words of Zephaniah 3:17, God turns down the volume on our fears as he "quiets us by his love."

Paul goes on to say, "We put no obstacle in anyone's way, so that no fault may be found with our ministry, but as servants of God we commend ourselves in every way: by great endurance, in afflictions, hardships, calamities..." (2 Cor 6:3—4). Because we're safe in the Father's love, we're freed up to work with every fiber of our being to be trustworthy friends to those far from God—to be the kind of people who can be counted on by people far from God. We're freed up to be the kind of men and women who don't pack up and go home at the first sign of trouble, hardship, or distress.

In fact, Paul demonstrates what this kind of resilience looks like, "We have spoken freely to you, Corinthians; our heart is wide open... In return... widen your hearts also" (2 Cor 6:11—13). Paul is saying he's done with living self-protectively. He's done living with a self-orientation.

There is a kind of vulnerability we can now model for the sake of Jesus, where we can be hurt, but still hold our hearts open. Where we can experience ingratitude from people, and still move towards them. We can't guarantee we'll never fail again. We can't guarantee we'll never experience ingratitude again. We can't guarantee we'll never be lied to again. We can't guarantee we'll never be hurt or disappointed again. But if we're willing to follow Jesus anyway, he can take the smallest speck of willingness, add the Spirit's power, and do eternally significant things in the lives of our "three."

A GUIDE TO PRAYING FOR EACH OTHER

A GUIDE TO PRAYING FOR EACH OTHER

An important way we can offer ourselves to God and each other is through prayer. Most Christians are familiar with praying their own thoughts for others. However, one of the best ways we can serve each other is through listening prayer. In listening prayer, we do not merely pray our own thoughts, but also allow God's Spirit to prompt and guide our prayers (1 Cor 14:3—4, 29—33, 39). If listening prayer is new for you, don't worry—it's probably new for others in the room as well. Here are eight guidelines:

1. Start by asking if anyone would like to receive prayer. If no one volunteers, invite someone. (Are you yourself facing something hard? Take a risk and request prayer!)

2. Place a chair in the middle of the room, and then ask permission to lay hands on the person. As a general rule, when laying hands on someone of the opposite gender, keep your hands above the shoulders.

3. Pray briefly to invite the Holy Spirit's presence to bless, speak, and act. Then quietly listen to the Lord together for at least 60 seconds.

4. After you have taken time to listen, if any Scriptures, pictures, thoughts, or gut impressions come to mind, share them with the person, and then pray briefly in light of what you shared.

5. Share tentatively and humbly. Avoid grand pronouncements or definitive language like "God is telling me..." Instead, you might say, "I have a sense..." or "I felt prompted to pray for..."

6. Encourage those who might be feeling reluctant to share. You might quietly ask each other, "Are you getting anything?" Pastor and author Sam Storms reminds us to "make room and time... for people to express what God has laid on their heart... [I]t's okay to fail or to miss it... [N]o one will be judged or excluded or laughed at if they don't always hit the nail on the head."

7. Take a moment to debrief with the person who received prayer. You might ask, "Did any of that particularly stand out to you?" or "Did any of that feel particularly meaningful or accurate?" You might then ask each other a similar question as a broader group.

8. Finally, as a rule, what you share should be encouraging or comforting. Avoid sharing anything negative or critical. If you feel that God has brought something corrective, sensitive, or potentially life-altering to your mind, find a time to share privately with one of your leaders and let them decide on the appropriate response. To be clear, refrain from sharing about "mates, dates, babies, or moves" or other potentially life-altering circumstances.

Made in the USA
Columbia, SC
11 February 2023

11654309R00043